151

Quick Ideas to Motivate Your Sales Force

151

Quick Ideas to Motivate Your Sales Force

Frank R. Horvath
and
Julie A. Vincent

CAREER
PRESS
The Career Press, Inc.
Franklin Lakes, NJ

151 QUICK IDEAS TO MOTIVATE YOUR SALES FORCE
EDITED BY KATE HENCHES
TYPESET BY MICHAEL FITZGIBBON
Cover design by Jeff Piasky
Printed in the U.S.A. by Book-mart Press

To order this title, please call toll-free 1-800-CAREER-1 (NJ and Canada: 201-848-0310) to order using VISA or MasterCard, or for further information on books from Career Press.

The Career Press, Inc., 3 Tice Road, PO Box 687,
Franklin Lakes, NJ 07417
www.careerpress.com

Library of Congress Cataloging-in-Publication Data
Horvath, Frank R.
151 quick ideas to motivate your sales force / by Frank R. Horvath and Julie A. Vincent.
   p. cm.
      Includes index.
      ISBN 978-1-60163-049-0
      1. Sales management. 2. Employee motivation. I. Vincent, Julie A.
   II. Title. III. Title: One hundred fifty-one quick ideas to motivate your sales force.

   HF5438.4.H67 2009
   658.8'1--dc22

2008035824

Contents

How to Use This Book

Every quick idea in this book is tested and true. They come from the collected experiences and wisdom of literally hundreds of people—well beyond just the authors. And they are presented here to help you learn how better to make high-quality decisions and to learn the best practices in delegating.

The book is designed to be consumed piecemeal—that is, in small bites. So don't try all of these ideas all at once. Read the book through to gain a quick impression of the ideas here, then start picking out those that seem to you to be immediately helpful, and try them out. They are the ones that can make a quick difference. Later, review the book again and try some additional ideas.

Of course, some of these ideas are in sequence, and those will be obvious and will make logical sense to you when you read them. Later, go back and review the others routinely and pick a few more to try. And so on...

So, at first read, label the ideas you read as:

- Implement now.
- Review in a month.
- Review later.
- Pass idea on to _____.

15

Every 90 days or so revisit the book for some new ideas or techniques. As your situation changes, you may well find usable ideas that you discounted earlier.

Remember, all of these ideas and concepts are proven techniques—proven by research and other professionals around the country and around the world. They have worked for others, and they can work for you!

Introduction

Ever think the only way to motivate your sales force is with money? That might work for a short while, but think again. There are more lasting ways to motivate your sales professionals, and that's where this book will motivate *you* to think long term, with the goal of engaging and retaining those top-notch sales employees.

151 Quick Ideas to Motivate Your Sales Force contains useful and practical ideas to keep enthusiasm and pride in your sales department—everything from how to develop your sales professionals to how to fire a customer. It discusses how to stretch goals and objectives, how to set up a scoreboard of sales results, and how to define clear accountabilities.

This book also talks about subjects not often found in sales manuals (the human behavior side of the business) such as how to use failure as a learning tool, how to establish a mentoring program, and even how to shed the "strip club mentality."

In today's economy, hitting those sales goals is a must. And we all know how expensive it is to carry a sales associate who doesn't pull his or her weight, and lose those who do. For example, do you take the time and effort to understand the family dynamics of your sales professionals? Your sales professionals are human beings, and they are influenced by their families and by what's going on in their lives at any given time. Done correctly, it can be helpful to get to know your sales team members on a deeper level.

151 Quick Ideas to Motivate Your Sales Force discusses sales from the company's perspective, from the manager's perspective, and from the sales professional's perspective. The result is a unique blend of practical suggestions to help your sales associates relish business opportunities and share in the success.

In short, everybody wins when you have a stable, talented, and motivated sales force. In today's world, the stakes are high. So start reading and see how far you can take your sales team. Take a minute to remember when you were a new sales professional ready to take on the world. Help your team become more successful, celebrate the wins, and contribute to the future. The time is now.

1

Share and Make Sure Sales Professionals Understand the Realities of Your Business

One of the biggest assumptions sales leaders and managers make is that sales professionals really understand how the business operates and how it makes a profit. *Do not assume* everyone understands the realities of your business. Ask yourself, do sales professionals understand how you make a profit and what's important to your operations? How about competitive intelligence? Have you researched and collected current competitor information that can be shared? Do they understand your income statement, balance sheet, and cash flows? How about your strategy, business brand, and key goals and objectives?

Assignment

Begin inserting financial operating metrics and competitive intelligence into your regular meetings with your sales professionals. Also use one-on-one conversations as an opportunity to share what the business is focused on, including the impact to sales, cash flow, and profitability.

Epilogue

The best sales professionals relish opportunities to share in the realities of your business. This enables them to sustain a competitive advantage when selling against overly optimistic sales competitors.

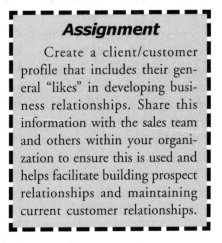

Align Your Sales Professionals to the "Likes" of the Customer/Client

This is about relationships that your sales professionals *want* to have with the customers/clients, and not about the fluffy "likes" that unskilled sales professionals put stock in as those that work with their customers and clients. Customers and clients know what they "like" in a business relationship. Sometimes it's purely transactional—and they only want to purchase your product/service at the lowest possible price. A relationship doesn't matter.

Assignment

Create a client/customer profile that includes their general "likes" in developing business relationships. Share this information with the sales team and others within your organization to ensure this is used and helps facilitate building prospect relationships and maintaining current customer relationships.

On the flip side and most important side of the sales process, it's your sales professional and her/his relationship that matters. It's also about the investment he/she makes in solving a business problem. Skills and competencies associated with your sales staff will have to be matched to the "likes" (or, defined differently, "preferences") of the customer/client. Customers and clients don't know what they don't like. It will take extra effort for your sales professionals to uncover the "likes" or "preferences" as part of their relationships, when they buy products and services or solve their business problems. Customers/clients are also likely to pay extra, or value the relationship more when their "likes" and their needs as an organization are matched to the sales professional.

20

People don't like to feel as though they are being sold. Rather, they like the opportunity to make decisions about their purchases. Coach your sales professionals to focus on allowing your clients and prospects to feel that they are the ones making the buying decision. You will experience a marked increase in closed.

Epilogue

Business relationships grow when you understand how your customers "like" to buy, not to be sold. Being sold imakes your client decline a sale.

3

Collect Feedback From Your Customers/Clients for Improvement

Improvement in your sales performance is an ongoing task. This is a motivational factor imbedded in the DNA of all top sales professionals. Your support in collecting constructive feedback will not only be welcome, but also will be a demonstration that you

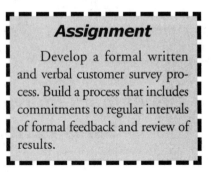

Assignment

Develop a formal written and verbal customer survey process. Build a process that includes commitments to regular intervals of formal feedback and review of results.

are truly trying to comprehend the process of feedback—not just for the sake of collecting feedback, but for the importance of learning how to improve the sales process. This translates into a motivating factor for your sales professionals. This should be a major priority, but don't get confused about only collecting feedback from your sales team. Sharing objective feedback also builds confidence in your customer relationships. By doing this on a regular and routine basis, your sales team will understand that it is an important part of their jobs to provide you with important feedback that they hear from their customers/clients. Used correctly with your sales team, feedback can also be tied to formal individual and team performance coaching.

If the information is handled constructively, your sales team will use it as a motivator to solve customer problems, address customer inquiries and complaints, and be willing to proactively provide you with a continuous loop of constructive process improvement-focused feedback. Along with your expectation to provide collected feedback on a regular basis, this will facilitate a continuous improvement philosophy for your sales team's ongoing growth and development as sales professionals.

Epilogue

Feedback is the cornerstone of sales process improvement. This applies to your customers/clients as well as your sales team.

4

Benchmark Individual and Team Sales Performance

It's true that what you measure gets done, and top-notch sales professionals want to be benchmarked. This is the only way a top professional gets motivated—by going above and beyond goals and objectives that have been set for past performance! Sales professionals are motivated by their ability to beat and exceed sales targets. Once these targets are set and agreed to, a top-notch sales professional will exhibit behaviors that coordinate her/his time and daily activities to beat and exceed sales goals and targets. Also remember that benchmarking sales metrics for performance allows you to see gaps in performance that need to be addressed. In addition to increasing individual motivation, benchmarking can provide you, as the manager, visibility into the benchmarks your competition uses and perspective on how to beat them.

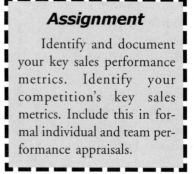

Assignment

Identify and document your key sales performance metrics. Identify your competition's key sales metrics. Include this in formal individual and team performance appraisals.

Take note as a sales manager: Your competition benchmarks their performance against yours. Your sales professionals are also knowledgeable about what's expected of their competitors' sales teams.

Epilogue

Because it's in a sales professional's DNA to be motivated by metrics, goals, and objectives, benchmark their performance in order to help them understand how their performance stacks up.

5

Align Sales With All Departments

Don't be a sales manager novice. If you want to be the best, then keep in mind that sales planning, budgeting, and forecasting must align with all the resource requirements of marketing, finance, operations, customer service, and manufacturing. This should be one of your major priorities on a recurring and annual basis. This also needs to be an ongoing part of sales operations management during any given fiscal year. As you align your sales process to the rest of the business,

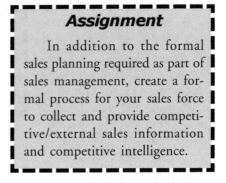

Assignment

In addition to the formal sales planning required as part of sales management, create a formal process for your sales force to collect and provide competitive/external sales information and competitive intelligence.

also think about sales force intelligence-gathering and how the information you gather about your competition can be incorporated to help the rest of your organization perform better. The information collected by your sales team needs to be collected in a formal way, and continuously shared so that this information can be incorporated into communications with key operations of the business. Salespeople love to acquire, and are motivated by acquiring lots of intelligence about their competition—their paychecks depend on it. Use the assignment here to include your sales team in the intelligence-gathering process. It assists in building a strong relationship with your sales team.

Epilogue

Sales professionals want to win and contribute to the ongoing sustainability of the company.

Set Sales Goals That Are a "Stretch," Not Realistic

Mediocrity kills sales performance. Some sales professionals "sandbag." Top-notch sales professionals are motivated by their ability to achieve and acquire more, more, more. If you want sales performance to be the best, and you want to highly motivate your sales team, it's time to think about going beyond what is realistic and create and lead sales goals that are truly a "stretch."

> ### Assignment
> *Do not* be afraid to set "stretch" goals and objectives for your sales professionals. They relish wanting to achieve, and achieve to a higher level. Review your current performance and compensation plan. Identify areas for sales performance improvement and set the expected targeted performance. Include pay incentives to achieve the targets.

Most sales professionals also set goals for themselves that are higher than what you set for them. Ask for and have a continuous dialogue with your sales professionals about their goals and objectives, and what you have set for them to accomplish. You might also want to consider reviewing your compensation program so that you have the ability to stretch opportunities, not just meeting "realistic" goals and objectives.

> ### Epilogue
> *Set the "stretch goals" and coach vigorously to help your sales professionals accomplish their goals. Watch them relish the challenge.*

7

Develop a Specific Sales Plan That Is Communicated to Everyone in the Organization

Beyond your sales team, the rest of the organization has a strong desire to understand how the business is growing through increases in sales and new customers. Not to be trite or simplistic just for simplicity purposes, but, as the sales manager, you need to communicate

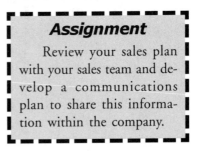

Assignment

Review your sales plan with your sales team and develop a communications plan to share this information within the company.

your sales plan with the rest of the organization. The key word is "communicate." As you share this information, you will find that your sales professionals love that they can bond with the rest of the organization by sharing their plans, goals, and objectives, and how they contribute to making the organization successful. Your sales professionals want people to know what they do and how they perform. This keeps them in the game and accountable. Sales professionals tap into the internal social networks of your organization, and test the knowledge of other people to see if it is in tune with how they are performing.

Epilogue

Sales professionals believe they are the "lifeblood" of the organization. They want to know that other people in the company care about their contribution to generate revenue.

Fire Bad Customers/Clients

There's no question about it. Do the math. Bad customers cost you money. While dedicating a larger portion of my career to being a sales professional, I calculated my time, energy, and effort spent working with a bad customer. My manager didn't have the intestinal fortitude to fire our bad customers/clients, so I

> **Assignment**
>
> Review the profitability of all your customers. Identify the bottom 5 percent. Collect feedback on customer relationships from your sales team. If you have customers at 5 percent or less, along with a poor relationship rating—*fire them!*

felt trapped, unproductive, and financially accountable for the time I was wasting in working with a customer who drove our operations and customer service professionals crazy! As a sales manager leading a 7team of professionals, it's your obligation to calculate opportunity costs/losses for not spending more time with your best customers and/or prospects.

Epilogue

Bad customers drain your bottom line and alienate your top sales professionals. Fair warning! If you do not have a method in place for firing your bad customers, your sales team will get frustrated and move on to your competition.

9

Keep Abreast of Industry Trends and Share the Information With Your Team

Self-development is a key competency that the majority of managers do not exhibit. Top sales professionals want to work for a sales manager who dedicates the time and energy to be a "thought leader." As someone who keeps abreast of industry trends and shares this information, you demonstrate your commitment to their continued knowledgebase, drive to comprehend new related business information, and learning.

Assignment

Become an avid reader and researcher about your industry. Share one key learning experience a week with your sales team. Demonstrate the behavior of your personal self-development and your commitment to your team's individual and collective learning and development.

Epilogue

Sales professionals are avid learners. They also want to keep up on industry trends so that they can turn this information into sales opportunities with their best customers.

10

Conduct an Annual Sales Conference Reviewing Past Sales Performance and Future Sales Plans

This does not have to be a huge drain on your annual budget or a blowout at some fancy resort. Sales professionals want to gather with their colleagues on a regular basis. At a minimum, if you are managing a virtual sales force, plan to meet at

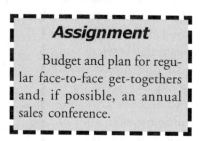

Assignment

Budget and plan for regular face-to-face get-togethers and, if possible, an annual sales conference.

least once a year for updates on sales performance, company performance, and social networking opportunities. Don't forget the all-important opportunity to provide accolades for a job well done. Accomplishments that are privately and publicly recognized go a long way for sales professionals as they acquire rewards for their successes. While you have your team together in one place, it is helpful and productive to include the communication of your future sales plan and direction of the company so that everyone who is participating in your conference hears the same messages.

Epilogue

Sales professionals have a need to celebrate their successes and hear how they can contribute to future plans for the company.

11

Focus on Customer Service

Head out to your nearest bookseller and check out the books in the business section. If you look for the topic of customer service, you will find hundreds of books that focus on it and authors who continue to make a lot of money trying to teach companies and sales professionals how to provide the best. *Here's the real deal:* Ask and an-

> ### Assignment
>
> Define your customer service philosophy and set high standards for delivering exceptional customer service in addition to closing deals. Incorporate the evaluation of customer service in your reward and compensation plans. Use this as a benchmark when evaluating performance. Also include the evaluation of customer service skills when you have the need to hire sales professionals.

swer this question...when's the last time you experienced top-notch service in the sales process? I'll bet you can't remember the last time you encountered a sales professional with the skills to deliver top-notch service along with getting the business. Close the deal and move on; that's the way sales professionals have been taught. Here's some "secret sauce" for you as a sales manager: top-notch sales professionals objectively put themselves in their customers' shoes. They evaluate all internal responses from and to your customers. Teach your sales professionals the "art of outstanding customer service in addition to closing the deal." This will not only develop respect and integrity with your sales professionals, but will also have an impact that will delight your customers. Watch the motivation rise as your sales professionals bond with your customers, and see the increase in revenue that you require to grow and sustain your business.

Epilogue

When you define and expect behavior that supports exceptional customer service, your sales professionals will follow suit.

12

Develop Business Case Studies That Demonstrate Competitive Value

Your sales team and your customers are motivated by business success! Can you demonstrate the competitive value and a compelling business case related to your products and services? Hopefully you can. Business case studies demonstrate your ability to provide competitive value. Sales professionals who can ensure that their customers/clients have successful customer

Assignment

Document business/product/ service case studies that demonstrate your ability to create value, solve a complex business problem, and deliver for your customers. Use this information for new prospects. Keep this information fresh and quantitative. Demonstrate your capability to either increase a prospect's top-line or bottom-line results.

experiences, realize a tremendous need to defend the success that your organization and team have delivered. The translation of your products/services into real-life case studies enables the use of critical competitive information that supports your sales team's sales efforts.

Quantitative and qualitative business cases facilitate a sales professional's ability to demonstrate the competitive differences your company can bring to bear on delivering value, solving business problems, and selling products/solutions.

Epilogue

Top-notch sales professionals want to work for and contribute to a successful organization. Make it a priority to develop and share this type of information.

Create a "Virtual Bench" of Sales Professionals

What is a "virtual bench"? A "virtual bench" is a list of potential top-notch sales professionals that you might keep in the top drawer of your desk, just in case one of your top performers decides to leave your organization. Having this list of potential candidates is like having a regular and recurring "draft

Assignment

Make it a priority to have your sales professionals identify the top five sales people they know, and keep their profiles and resumes on hand as part of your succession plan for your sales team.

selection" list, and not having to wait until the draft begins once a year. This is one of the most significant business problems that companies face today—not having a bench and/or stable of competent professionals they can call on if they have turnover. Talent bench shortfall is one of four factors within management's control to fix. Be a leader and key your eye on a virtual bench for sales professionals. Even if your turnover is low and you have a highly productive sales force, you can keep valuable information on hand with regard to talent in the marketplace that can be inserted into your organization on a moment's notice, in the event you have unexpected turnover.

Epilogue

Top-notch sales professionals know other top-notch sales professionals. The social networking that ties top performers together will continue, as sales professionals gravitate to others inside and outside their professional industries.

14

Maintain Competitive Benchmark Information for Compensation

This is and should be obvious for sales managers who are keeping and retaining top-notch sales talent or who struggle with having to compete in today's competitive war for it. Competitive compensation to keep your sales team intact and motivated is a must in today's economy. Remember—you get what you pay for! Pay below average and you will get less than average or average performance. If you pay a little more for top-notch salespeople, my experience is that you will attract and retain higher-caliber sales professionals. Here's a sales myth I would like for you to think about: The only way to pay sales professionals and to motivate them is to pay them on commission. Sales professionals talk, and compare salaries and incentives. They know what their competition is paying. Collect market information on

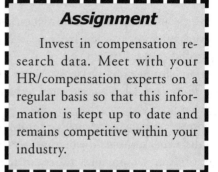

Assignment

Invest in compensation research data. Meet with your HR/compensation experts on a regular basis so that this information is kept up to date and remains competitive within your industry.

pay, and keep this up to date. Your sales professionals are.

Sales professionals are highly competitive and determine their value based on the drive to acquire more money and accomplish their goals and objectives they meet and the corresponding compensation they make.

Epilogue

Don't underestimate how sales professionals "level set" compensation as they compare their income to that of their colleagues and their competition.

15

Maintain Competitive Benchmark Information to Help Manage Performance

As high achievers, sales professionals want to defend their performance. They do this by comparing productivity, tasks, sales activities, and results to those around them and against whom they compete—peers in their industry and market space. In addition to individual performance, believe it or not, when you hire and have on your team top-performing sales professionals, they do have an innate sense of camaraderie and teaming in order to accomplish overall

> ### *Assignment*
>
> Try to collect as much performance and benchmark data as you can get your hands on...use this information to coach your sales professionals, set performance targets, reward top performance and align your sales objectives as they support your overall business strategy.

goals and objectives. Successful individual contributors, managers, and teams, although highly competitive, are also interested in determining how they are performing. Collect and keep up-to-date competition performance benchmark data.

> ### Epilogue
>
> *Use the competitive benchmark information not as a hammer but as a tool to motivate and support continuous improvement and the defense of your overall competitive landscape.*

16

Hire Top-Notch Sales Talent Outside Your Industry

Let's address the two ways to hire and/or "buy" sales talent. One way is to buy the talent within your industry. You want to acquire a proven sales talent and poach the intellectual property that the sales talent can bring into the organization. Here's a *revolutionary* approach that can change your business and your sales efforts: Smart sales managers are now "leap-frogging" their competition because they are hiring outside of their

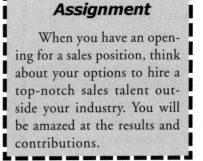

Assignment

When you have an opening for a sales position, think about your options to hire a top-notch sales talent outside your industry. You will be amazed at the results and contributions.

industries and/or competitive markets. Why? The learning is that top-notch sales performance and track records for delivering results are transferable to multiple industries and market spaces. Just focusing on hiring and buying sales talent within your industry might not be the smartest thing to do. When you have an opening for a top sales position, consider candidates that are outside your industry. Industry knowledge is important; however, successful sales competencies that are transferable are *more* important. All top-notch sales talent, are great learners. They will compress the learning curve to understand your industry and sell. Period.

Epilogue

Think about human DNA. The more incestuous you are, the less likely you are to generate new "genes" to enter your collective team. In this case, new "genes" translates to new ideas!

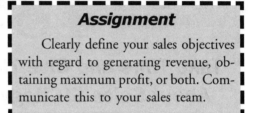

Profit vs. Revenue: Understand Your Sales Objectives

Sales managers focus on delivering to the top line of any business they lead. No secrets here. The defining difference is creating clarity for your sales team so

> **Assignment**
>
> Clearly define your sales objectives with regard to generating revenue, obtaining maximum profit, or both. Communicate this to your sales team.

that they can be focused on aligning your cash-generation options while your business is going through different business cycles. Are you trying to grow as fast as you can and generate skyrocketing revenue? Or are you trying to accomplish different objectives at different times of the business life cycle? Are you a "start-up" trying to generate revenue at a reasonable profit, or are you a more mature business trying to generate sustainable revenue and maximize profitability? As a sales manager, be clear about your objectives so that your team of motivated sales professionals can accomplish their task of acquiring what you are asking of them.

What motivates a top sales performer is the desire to acquire cash in the form that you have determined is in the best interests of growing and/or sustaining your business objectives. Don't make this complex. We all know that profit is king, but you many have other expectations that will drive cash generation, team motivation, and individual deal behavior.

> **Epilogue**
>
> *Your sales team wants clear definition of your sales objectives. This will help guide them in their decision-making when working with customers and closing deals.*

18

Take Time and Give Time to Think About Sales Strategy and Plans

Want to really motivate your sales team? Don't give them more tasks to complete. Give them time to *think*! Brain power is generating more revenue and profit. Work less on sales administrative activities and give your sales professionals the time to really think about how to solve

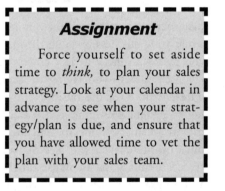

Assignment

Force yourself to set aside time to *think,* to plan your sales strategy. Look at your calendar in advance to see when your strategy/plan is due, and ensure that you have allowed time to vet the plan with your sales team.

their customers' business problems. Set aside enough time during the day and week to really think about your sales strategy and plans. As the saying goes, "fail to plan, plan to fail." This is also true in not allowing enough time to think about solving a customer's business problem. As is typical, you should invest the time to plan your strategy and execute your plan given the talent on your sales team. Allowing time to *think* and having the ability to articulate your thoughts to your sales team will be greatly appreciated and well received.

Epilogue

Understand that every day you are knee deep in "alligators and assholes" it's difficult to plan time to plan. You must *pull yourself away from the daily grind and set aside time to think.*

19

Establish and Communicate Your Sales and Marketing Brand

Your sales team wants to really understand your brand. Why is this important, and what does it have to do with the motivation of your sales professionals? They identify with your brand. A compelling business brand is something to be proud of, and reflects on

> **Assignment**
>
> Meet with your marketing team and/or decision-makers to clearly and concisely communicate your brand to your sales team.

what I've heard in interviews (and have advised sales executives about) as the "swagger." Whether it's a new sales hire or someone who's been with you for a long time, he or she will identify with your brand and demonstrate his or her loyalty to it by being proud to represent it.

Epilogue

Sales professionals establish their identities and come to work for you every day based on their belief in the brand that they are selling.

20

Ensure Everyone Understands Your Compelling Value Proposition

What is your compelling value proposition? Your sales team wants to know. In addition to comprehending and understanding your value proposition, salespeople have an innate drive to naturally defend something we care deeply about. We know that it is in the best interests of the organization and customers/clients that are served. Sales professionals want to know the "ins and outs" of the details of what they can offer and sell, and what customers are willing to pay for. Have you defined them? Can you quantify the value that your product and/or services have for an organization? Define your value proposition from information your sales team has collected regarding customer feedback and what your company offers as a competitive differentiator.

Assignment

Meet with your sales team to collect intelligence as to why customers buy from you. Translate this into the compelling value, meaning quantitative results that you sell and can offer companies to solve their business problems. Put this in writing and provide it as a tool for your sales team.

Epilogue

Customers want compelling value—reduced costs and/or increased revenue.

21

Validate Your Brand With Your Customer/Client Base

Your brand is important, and your sales professionals have an emotional tie to your brand. Always remember this—your competition does. This is a reason to validate your brand, but a more important one to ensure that your sales team has an emotional and intellectual connection to your brand. Ask your customers, clients, and sales professionals how they perceive your brand. This includes understanding the value proposition, how you stack up to your competition and any new products and services. Customers who are engaged with you as partners are the best sources of information on whether your brand is making an impact in the market.

> ### *Assignment*
> Assign your sales force to collect information about how your customers are "receiving and perceiving your marketplace brand." Collect the information, validate it, and provide it to your sales team and company decision makers.

> ### Epilogue
> *Your sales professionals who are in the field and meeting with customers day in and day out are your best source for collecting and validating branding information. This includes whether you are hitting or missing the target with your customers.*

Be Realistic About Sales Goals

Being realistic does not mean "sandbagging" the sales goals. This is not to say that realistic goals can't be "stretch" goals as mentioned in Quick Idea #6. You can be realistic about your sales target and still set goals that stretch you out of your comfort zone.

Assignment

Whether you are setting annual, quarterly, monthly, weekly, or daily sales goals, obtain input from your sales team, vet the sales goals against your business strategy, and then set the goals that give you the best opportunity to successfully accomplish your sales/business objectives.

Top-notch sales professionals typically set higher personal goals than do their sales managers and/or senior management.

Respect comes from being "realistic"—in other words, communicating with your team in a straightforward manner. "Here are our goals. We understand our mission to accomplish these goals. This is what's expected of you to help achieve these goals, and I will hold you accountable to deliver." As you share this message with your sales professionals, also include vetting sales goals with your sales team, and you will get the buy-in necessary to reach your goals, regardless of timetables.

Epilogue

Randomly assigned sales goals are typically not grounded in reality, nor are they defined as "stretch" goals. When you are realistic as a sales manager, you will gain your sales professionals' respect.

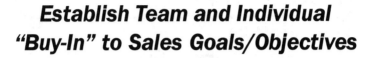

Establish Team and Individual "Buy-In" to Sales Goals/Objectives

Once you've established realistic sales goals, then the next step in the process is to obtain "buy-in" from your sales team. The buy-in creates self-accountability in exceeding established goals. So you have taken the advice of being realistic and also establishing

> **Assignment**
>
> First, be sure everyone on your sales team understands what performance expectations are for the organization, your sales team, and individual sales contributors. Regularly conduct meetings with your sales team to establish goals, align them to your business strategy, and establish the metrics by which you determine your progress.

"stretch" goals. Nice job. As mentioned in Quick Idea #22, your next step is to establish the "collective buy-in" on organizational goals, specific team goals for sales, and individual goals that contribute to the goals that support both team and organizational success.

The advantages of buy-in or what I define as collaboration with "non-negotiables" (accountabilities, skills, and performance expectations that are must-haves in the job to be successful), greatly outweigh the "old-school, 1950s dictatorial" approach that the sales manager has all the answers, sets the goals/objectives, and knows all the answers to achieving said goals.

> ### Epilogue
> *Trust that your sales team is bright, ambitious, and willing to invest and buyin to their own individual accomplishments and those of the team.*

24

Buy Shares of Stock in Your Customers/Clients

There's no better position to be in than to be the owner. When you have a stake in the success of your company, shit happens—period. People want to be successful, and top performers hate to

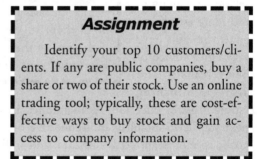

Assignment

Identify your top 10 customers/clients. If any are public companies, buy a share or two of their stock. Use an online trading tool; typically, these are cost-effective ways to buy stock and gain access to company information.

lose and fail. If your customers/clients are public companies, then, by all means, buy a share or two of their stock. In addition to being able to proclaim that you are an owner and have a stake in the business (even if it's minimal), you will receive a wealth of information about their past performance and future business plans. Additionally, past customer performance may give you clues to business problems you and your sales team can offer to fix. Remember, in addition to sales activities to uncover sales opportunities, there might be a smarter and faster way to get to the information you need to *think* about to create sales leads and opportunities. Future business plans will give you the fuel for upcoming solutions to their expected future business direction.

> ### Epilogue
> *Ownership and investment demonstrate you have "skin in the game." They also give you huge opportunities to coach and assist your sale professionals in taking a serious role in acquiring information and defending their ownership. Pretty powerful motivation tools!*

25

When Forecasting Sales Numbers, Forecast Reality, and Be Conservative

Teach your sales professionals to forecast their sales numbers realistically. Nothing is more *demotivating* than getting all pumped up about aggressive and optimistic sales numbers that dont materialize. Be careful. The temptation to over-forecast can come back to

> ### Assignment
> Vet all forecasted sales numbers against what you have managerial control over, along with the factors that you don't control.

bite you. There is nothing worse than to have to go to your boss or drill into your team because your sales projections were not done properly. Outside of your managerial control are four factors:

1. Regulatory actions.
2. Economic downturn.

3. Geopolitical changes.

4. National labor market inflexibility.

Other than that, all other business factors—both strategic and organizational—are under your control. Be thoughtful in the forecasting process, and, as the old sales saying goes: "It's better to under promise and over-deliver."

Epilogue

When forecasts are not properly vetted, reality gets distorted. If you do not take a realistic and conservative approach, the results of your forecast might find you looking for another job.

26

Define Clear Accountabilities

Job descriptions, roles, and responsibilities might be formal human resources documents used in the hiring and performance management processes, but typically this information is not included in human resources documentation.

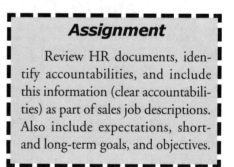

Assignment

Review HR documents, identify accountabilities, and include this information (clear accountabilities) as part of sales job descriptions. Also include expectations, short- and long-term goals, and objectives.

Specific and *clear* accountabilities, performance expectations, and short- and long-term goals and objectives must be defined by the hiring manager or sales leader. Sales professionals who are clear about their accountabilities, expectations, goals, and objectives perform at a higher level than those who aren't sure about their expectations. Top-notch sales performers expect to be measured for success.

Epilogue

Sales professionals measure their career success through the direct measurement of accountabilities. A sure way to obtain high levels of performance is to be crystal clear about sales accountabilities. A sure way to demotivate a career-minded sales professional is to be unclear about accountabilities.

27

Hold Sales Professionals to Clear Accountabilities

Sales professionals want to be held to standards—"accountabilities." By doing this, you can accomplish two very important underlying drives. The first is to really understand what needs to be ac-

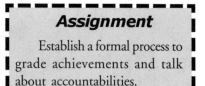

Assignment

Establish a formal process to grade achievements and talk about accountabilities.

complished (what the tasks are and what activities make up my accountabilities). The second is the drive to obtain my goal. I can only do this when I first understand with clarity the accountabilities that are expected of me as a sales professional. It's your job as the manager to define the accountabilities, set expectations for achievement, and then follow up to determine whether individuals and/or sales teams have gaps in performance or are exceeding expectations. In addition to the personal pressure they put on themselves, they also want regular and timely feedback from their sales manager.

> ### Epilogue
> *Sales professionals get up in the morning with a clear line of sight on what they want to accomplish and are accountable for, and how they can exceed expectations.*

28

Define and Assess Sales Competencies for Understanding Personal Strengths and Development Needs

A competency is a skill or behavior that is critical to be successful in your job. Many valid competency models exist in the marketplace. Competencies are the "common language" in setting develop-

Assignment

Research and select a sales competency such as the one described in Michael M. Lombardo and Robert W. Eichinger's book... Use this model to define sales skills/behaviors and assess current skills/behaviors of your sales team.

ment and performance assessments. If your human resources department has not already embarked on establishing this foundational information within the organization, then be the first leader to do so. Pick one. Ensure that the competency model has been validated and can withstand employment and legal compliance. Then define the sales skills/behaviors necessary to be a top sales performer. Use a competency at model such as the Lominger International at *www.lominger.com* and The Devine Group at *www.devinegroup.com* to assess the current skills of your sales team.

Epilogue

Don't use the generic and/or boilerplate sales job descriptions that come from the human resources department. Invest in a valid sales competency model. This is the platform you will use to recruit, hire, develop, and retain top-notch sales professionals.

29

Provide Regular, Consistent Feedback on Performance

Employee engagement surveys and the research I've conducted uncover that employees want and require regular and consistent feedback on their performance. The research also provides the insights that employees don't get regular, consistent feedback, and that most managers are horrible at this

Assignment

There are two assignments on this topic:

1. Invest in some managerial coaching on giving great performance feedback.
2. Create a simple form that includes all competencies and accountabilities for the job. Establish a formal process to provide regular feedback.

managerial task. Be a unique and different kind of sales manager. A top accountability for any sales manager is to provide regular, constructive, and consistent feedback on performance. "A-players" seek out regular feedback from their peers, coworkers, and clients/customers. A-players also expect to have candid and constructive coaching and feedback to improve performance from their bosses. Recent research conducted on employee engagement and retention clearly shows that the number-one reason for leaving a company is lack of managerial feedback and support.

Epilogue

If you do not provide regular, constructive, and consistent feedback, expect your top performance to become a turnover statistic for you.

30

Test Individual Sales Knowledge About Products, Services, Customers, and Competitors

There are three ways to test sales knowledge. One way is scenario testing that includes "real time" evaluation while on a sales call. This certainly is the best way to observe behaviors and knowledge about your products and services. The second is laboratory testing. This offers a safe environment for the learner to act in a similar way to a real-time sales call. If you cannot invest the time to regularly go with your sales professionals on real-time sales calls, this is a nice and effective alternative to understanding their knowledge base. The last, and least effective, is written "knowledge-based" testing. This can be, used for understanding a person's knowledge, and to directly grade his or her knowledge about products,

---

Assignment

Identify gaps in your training and development agenda for your sales force. Apply the testing techniques mentioned previously and correlate your training and development gaps. You can then target your development investments in order to close the gaps and improve individual and team sales performance.

---

services, customers, and competitors. All of these techniques will work to some degree.

Epilogue

The results of testing sales knowledge will identify the gaps in knowledge you need to close in order for sales professionals to perform at a higher level.

31

Recognize Top Performance With Regular Awards of Achievement

Sales awards are symbolic of accomplishment, achievement, and pride. This is the sales professional's desire to close more deals and compare our accomplishments of achievement to that of our peers and competition. When you regularly recognize top performance with a mix of awards, you will not only satisfy the sales professionals' needs to be motivated to achieve, but you will also be satisfying the

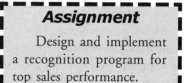

Assignment

Design and implement a recognition program for top sales performance.

organization's expectation to recognize top sales performance. Recognition of top performance must be a regular part of your sales manager's role and responsibility.

As sales managers of a regional distributor, we established a quarterly and annual sales recognition program for top revenue performance. This included name recognition for top quarterly sales performance on a sales plaque that hung in our front door lobby. On an annual basis, the top sales performers received cash incentive bonuses, recognition in our annual sales meeting by our president, and an engraved plaque that was represented in our company awards trophy case.

Epilogue

Top sales professionals chose this career for a living for two reasons: money, and recognition for a task well done. Status based on making more money and having more awards than anyone else is what's important to top sales performers.

32

Fire Nonperformers

I am not advocating that you administer the GE style of performance management whereby you weed out the bottom 10 percent of your workforce on an annual basis. What I am recommending, though, is that you take the first step to regularly address poor performance. This is a tough job and one that is difficult for all managers, especially sales managers. Remember, the first thing you need to do is to have defined sales competencies and accountabilities. As a sales manager, it's your job to compare performance to sales skills and competencies, along with expected accountabilities. When this is clear between you and your sales professionals, there is no question that when you observe and experience poor performance, you have a common platform and measuring stick. If you find poor performance, don't wait until an annual performance review. Extreme gaps

Assignment

Use your tool kit of sales competencies/skills and accountabilities to manage and/or uncover gaps in individual performance.

in performance must be addressed at any given moment and time.

If, as the sales leader, you do not address nonperformance, you will be asked to leave the organization. Your replacement will be asked to clean up nonperformance. Additionally, your top performers will not tolerate nonperformance. If you do not address this, your top performers will also exit the organization.

Epilogue
Nonperformance is the cancer within your organization and sales team.

33

Set the Expectation That Sales Professionals Understand the "Ins and Outs" of Their Customers/ Clients' Businesses

The "ins and outs" of your customers'/clients' businesses are where you can solve business problems. Intimate knowledge of business processes and pain points gives the sales professional the platform to identify, analyze, and recommend creative business solutions to your customers and clients. Sales professionals are highly motivated by trying to understand the world around them. Help

> **Assignment**
>
> Establish a customer profile sheet and assign your sales professionals to collect business process intelligence for all your customers/clients.

make their worlds bigger, and everyone wins. Understand your customers'/clients' businesses beyond just what you are selling. This demonstrates that you care to solve their business problems.

> **Epilogue**
> *Understanding and caring are hardwired in sales professionals. Leverage these emotions.*

When Evaluating Performance, Focus on Results, Not on Time

Results are the only things, that matter. Just like in professional sports, people get paid to perform, get results, and win. Bottom line: like the professional sports analogy, there is no place tougher and more difficult in business than sales. Everyone has visibility into whether you achieve your results, close deals, and win. Top sales performers measure their success by differentiating **great** performance and results from that of average or poor performance. Your sales professionals will also be manually calculating in their heads their performance versus the number of hours invested to close a deal. It may only matter if the time invested exceeds the deal itself. Exceptional performance by top-notch sales performance is evaluated from

a simple mathematical business formula of profit and loss. As a sales manager, focus on the "results equals deals closed"methodology and not on whether one of your sales professionals is signing in to a time clock. Also, remember that most deals are closed outside the normal course of business hours, so time is irrelevant in comparison to obtaining the ultimate objective of closing the deal.

Epilogue
Time is relevant only if the invested time exceeds the cost of the deal.

35

Set Up a Scoreboard of Sales Results

All sales performers keep score! They keep score in their heads, they review their weekly progress, and read management reports that compare their results to that of their peers. Do you have a visible scoreboard and track your sales results? Doesn't matter if it's in the office on a whiteboard or in an electronic scorecard—the point is to have your overall sales progress and results visible to your sales professionals and key people in your organization. Sales professionals understand that their performance is going to be measured and viewed by their peers, coworkers, and bosses. Top performers want to see, on a regular basis, how they compare to their peers. As you define

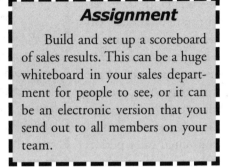

Assignment

Build and set up a scoreboard of sales results. This can be a huge whiteboard in your sales department for people to see, or it can be an electronic version that you send out to all members on your team.

expected competencies, accountabilities, and metrics, this becomes the scoreboard for performance comparison.

Epilogue

Some managers believe that creating into a scoreboard of sales results establishes unwanted internal competition. You must set the tone as the manager/leader of your sales team that this is a very positive way to give visibility to top performance. Your top performers will thank you.

36

Conduct Weekly Sales Status Calls With Your Sales Team

No matter whether you have a centralized or decentralized sales operation, you should conduct weekly updates with your team. You may be managing a group of sales professionals who report into an office and you get to see them on a consistent basis. You may be a sales manager who has to manage a team that is virtual and/or a combination of office and virtual sales professionals. By sharing timely sales information and having access to their sales manager to ask questions and collaborate with their peers, sales professionals get the connection to you as the manager and the ability to bond with their peers.

> ### *Assignment*
> Have an agenda to conduct face-to-face weekly meetings, conference calls, or both. Establish a recurring time once a week to give an update on business changes, sales successes, and goals for the upcoming week.

> ### Epilogue
> *Business changes fast. The only way to keep your sales professional informed and connected to the business is through constant recurring communications, whether face-to-face or via conference calls.*

37

Send a Handwritten Note for Outstanding Performance

Don't underestimate the power of personal attention to a job well done by someone on your team. We all might as well practice what we preach with regard to what clients/customers really love. What they love—and it's just human nature—is a personal touch. A handwritten note goes a long way to telling someone that you care about his or her contributions, growth, development, and outstanding performance.

Recognition provides the fuel for additional motivation to go beyond the call of duty, especially when the manager invests the time and energy to recognize outstanding perfor-

> ### Assignment
>
> Establish a routine to send personal notes to your top performers. Include your appreciation for their contributions and performance.

mance. Do it on a regular basis, and be sincere. You will see people smile and go beyond their normal performance.

Epilogue

Personal notes about outstanding performance will have a positive psychological impact on your sales contributors.

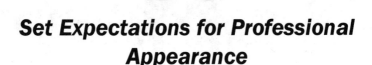

38

Set Expectations for Professional Appearance

It's true. People do judge your sales professionals' appearances. We all judge and size up someone we meet and/ or work with based on his or her professional appearance. Although

> ### Assignment
>
> Call your sales team together and decide what the expectations will be for professional appearance during sales calls and while on a customer site during a project.

some might argue to "when in Rome do as the Romans do," this is not what I am recommending in today's competitive business environment. Your sales professionals need to dress and present themselves as "A-players" with an "A-attitude." Appearance is reflected in an individual's mood and demeanor. Dress like a slob and chances are, your behavior is, at some point, going to reflect that appearance. At a minimum, your customers and clients will equate a sloppy appearance with an uncaring attitude. Customers/clients use first impressions and professional appearance as a sign of competence, right or wrong. Now, you can only hide behind professional appearance for so long if you don't have competence. But if you combine top-notch performance with top-notch professional appearance, you will beat your competition anytime you are face-to-face with your clients and customers.

> **Epilogue**
> Don't forget about human bias regarding appearance and looks.

39

Do Not Tolerate Bad Sales Behavior

What is bad sales behavior? Business professionals have certain standards and expectations when conducting business transactions. There are standards of

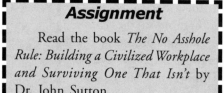

Assignment

Read the book *The No Asshole Rule: Building a Civilized Workplace and Surviving One That Isn't* by Dr. John Sutton.

behavior for ethics, integrity, and respect. These ally universally in business transactions, but are even more highly scrutinized in the conducting of sales transactions. Think of this in terms of what you expect as a sales leader and how this reflects on you personally. A lack of ethics, integrity, and respect reflects on you, your customers, and your team. While you are setting expectations for your team, your team will be watching how you, as the manager, respond if you have to address "bad sales behavior." Don't make it personal—just focus on the behaviors. If you don't address the bad behavior, I guarantee that you will lose your top sales professionals, because they hold themselves to high behavioral standards and won't tolerate a "wimpy" boss who does not address this.

> ### Epilogue
> *If you see, hear, or observe bad sales behavior, address it immediately and get all the facts. Once you have the facts, address the behavior.*

40

Don't Tolerate Excessive Drinking and Sales

Martini lunches are history. They used to be acceptable in the 1950s during our industrial and manufacturing heyday. Times have changed. Excessive drinking by sales professionals while they are working with your clients will come back to bite them.

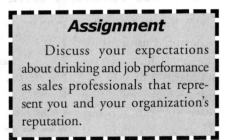

Assignment

Discuss your expectations about drinking and job performance as sales professionals that represent you and your organization's reputation.

It doesn't matter if you are conducting a luncheon meeting, on the golf course, or participating in a client dinner. Excessive drinking clouds the mental capacity to make sound business decisions. Period. It also clouds good judgment about what is or is not appropriate behavior in the sales process. Many sales professionals have watched their careers go down the drain when they think and behave like a fraternity or sorority member. This is not to say that all fraternity or sorority members drink excessively, but just think of their portrayal in *Animal House* and you will get the picture! Although some sales professionals are "old school" and may say this is the only way they could close the deal, don't believe them. Excessive drinking by your sales professionals can only lead you into a "boat load" (a business term I learned as an MBA) of credibility and legal risks.

> ### Epilogue
> *Social drinking, while in moderation, can be acceptable. Don't run the risk of tolerating excessive drinking by your sales team.*

41

Don't Tolerate the Strip Club Mentality

"My client wanted to go to the strip club and this is the only way I could close the deal." Deals for your business don't get closed in strip clubs. Other activities in the club take priority. Although this might be perceived or ar-

Assignment

As the sales manager, discuss your expectations about this type of customer entertainment. Review your company policies on business entertainment and understand them.

gued as a bonding and/or relationship-building exercise, the only thing being exercised is your pocket book as the sales manager. In today's business environment, many companies are developing (or have in place) policies about appropriate business entertainment and using company funds to conduct this type of deal closure or just entertaining a prospect. I've seen many sales managers (even with strip clubs being off limits in their company entertainment policy) get fired over allowing this type of behavior to exist on their teams. Although typically this is a male customer thing to do, don't be surprised if you have offended the other 50 percent of the workforce that is female.

> **Epilogue**
> *Strip club mentality has no place in today's business climate.*

42

Know When to Use the Carrot or the Stick

As a sales manager it's your job to understand when to use the carrot and when to use the stick. This is a simple and yet very complex concept. You first need to understand what personally motivates your sales

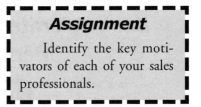

Assignment

Identify the key motivators of each of your sales professionals.

professionals. Do your sales professionals focus on building your business? Is the focus on building relationships? Are they at the beginning of their career, and you are developing their skills to really know how they can succeed? Or are they helping to protect your business and focusing on customer service? The difference between the two methods is motivation.

The carrot is a positive way to motivate, for example, with encouragement, coaching, and enthusiasm all meant to obtain an improved outcome. Some sales professionals respond better to the carrot. On the other hand, the stick is a constructive and sometimes negative way to motivate, for example with direct conversations about poor performance, or telling sales professionals that they won't obtain their sales goals. I find that individuals are wired to respond to and are motivated by either the carrot or stick—80 percent to the carrot and 20 percent to the stick. Effective sales managers need to know the difference between both how they use the carrot or stick, and how their sales professionals are wired to respond to these motivational tools.

Based on your motivational factors and any given business situation, you must decide if the use of a carrot or stick is relevant. If it is relevant, then you must match the carrot or stick to the response or behavior you want to see changed.

Epilogue
When applying the carrot-or-stick approach, be sure to match it to the behavior you want to see changed, along with the motivators of that particular sales professional.

43

Treat Sales Professionals as Professionals

There is nothing worse than *not* being treated as a professional. If you have an amateur attitude and apply amateur managerial behaviors, you will obtain amateur results. So, when you are hiring, use my recommendation to evaluate your sales candidates according to the key competencies and accountabilities that make your sales professionals successful. Similarly, use the same performance-measuring tools for your existing sales team. You have top sales professionals, and they want to be treated as such. As you hold yourself to professional standards, apply this same accountability to your sales professionals making sure to do it with dignity, candor, and respect.

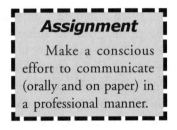

Assignment

Make a conscious effort to communicate (orally and on paper) in a professional manner.

The days of a command-and-control leadership style are over. Aathough this style worked in the 1950s, it does not work today. Sales professionals that are "A-players" expect to be treated in a respectful and equitable manner with regard to pay, incentives, ideas, contributions, and participation in solving business problems using their expertise and knowledge.

> **Epilogue**
> *If you have the command-and-control leadership style, you will lose top sales performers.*

44

Create Internal Competitions

Good, healthy internal competition fuels the soul. It also is a huge motivation for top sales performers t be considered the best among their peers. If you use a performance scoreboard as suggested in Quick Idea #35, and provide regular and consistent feedback

Assignment

Visibly tie your performance scoreboard and awards recognition initiatives into performance results. This will create healthy internal competitions for success.

and recognition awards, this will create a healthy process for competition within your sales team members. If you don't create healthy internal sales competitions, your sales team will create one of their own. Rather than having your sales team doing "off-track betting" on goals and objectives, set up regular, recurring, healthy, internal competitions so your sales professionals will be focused on your expected goals and objectives.

Epilogue
Internal competition is healthy, if handled correctly.

45

Create External Competitions

There are two choices here! You can define "external competitions" as

1. competitions with your competitors, or
2. from the perspective of outside your sales team and within your organization (for example, operations, finance, manufacturing).

Sales professionals like to know how they stack up with the competition as you have defined it previously, either as 1, 2, or

---

Assignment

Identify your competition's performance metrics and post them alongside your internal sales scoreboard. If you don't have access to external competitor performance metrics, then post and distribute internal functional operating metrics so you can compare your sales progress to what's important to the business.

---

both. External competition, if you have the data, is a great way to see how you are performing as compared to benchmarked sales data. Competition outside your sales team with other function areas gives you and your sales staff the opportunity to foster healthy competition related to common goals and objectives that support the overall business strategy.

Epilogue

Knowing and understanding your competition and internal function area performance metrics can create external competitions.

46

Put Your Sales Performers Into "A," "B," and "C" Categories

Don't consider this a normal distribution when you categorize your "A," "B," and "C" sales performers. "A" performers are those who always meet their sales targets, have high levels of sales competence, and

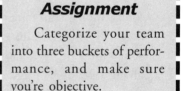

Assignment

Categorize your team into three buckets of performance, and make sure you're objective.

receive high performance marks for their service skills and problem resolution skills. "B" players need some development and learning to enhance their skill sets and achieve high motivation. A subset of "B" players does include the lazy ones who have high skills, but, for various reasons, lack the motivation to take their game to the next level and become an "A" player. "C" players have major gaps in competence and skill and rarely achieve their sales goals. Be sure you can categorize your sales performers correctly. Don't make this complicated. Keep it focused on competence, skills, and results related to accountabilities.

Epilogue

Sales managers have the accountability and responsibility to understand their team members' individual sales performance.

47

Do Everything You Can to Move Your "B" Sales Contributors to the "A" Level

What's the definition of a "B" sales contributor? When I've interviewed and worked with top sales executives and used sales competency assessment tools, I've found they are just like a typical grading scale

Assignment

Identify which category your "B" contributors fall into. Then either create a development plan to help build the necessary skills/competencies to make "A" contributors, or use the advice that's included in the "carrot-and-stick" approach to performance management.

contributor: They are operating in the 80-percent range. So the question is always, "How do I, as the sales manager, make an investment in moving my 'B' sales performers to the 'A' category?" First, you must understand that "B" sales contributors fall into two categories: they either need development or they are just plain lazy. Your job as the sales manager is to determine which of these categories a "B" sales contributor falls into. Be sure you're right. It's important.

> ### Epilogue
> *80 percent of your revenue comes from your sales performers. Any incremental change in "B" sales contributors will have incremental increases in your top-line revenue performance.*

48

Put Your "C" Sales Performers on a Performance Improvement Plan

Face the facts. When you have assessed your sales team for their level of competence and performance, they will all fit into one of three categories: "A" performers, "B" performers, and "C" performers. After you continue to coach and develop your "A" and "B" performers,

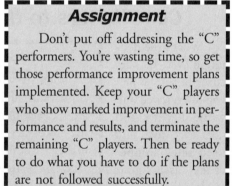

Assignment

Don't put off addressing the "C" performers. You're wasting time, so get those performance improvement plans implemented. Keep your "C" players who show marked improvement in performance and results, and terminate the remaining "C" players. Then be ready to do what you have to do if the plans are not followed successfully.

then you must turn your attention to and deal with your "C" sales performers. The bottom line is that "C" sales performers don't contribute the necessary levels of revenue, sometimes lack key skills sets necessary to perform at a higher level, and don't have the motivation to contribute at their highest level of performance.

Once you've identified your "C" performers, document a performance improvement plan that is specific to identified competencies, and accountabilities, including suggestions for improvement and a timeframe for a measured change in behavior and results.

Epilogue

Always keep in mind that you need a "virtual bench" of top sales performers.

Expect Sales Professionals to Have a Business Objective for Each and Every Sales Call

My review of top sales performers and their success uncovers that for every sales call a business objective is identified, communicated, and discussed with a customer/client. On the flip side, when sales professionals do *not* have a business ob-

> **Assignment**
>
> Set the performance expectation that every sales call must have a business objective. "A" performers do this as a routine. New sales performers may need coaching on the ways to establish a business objective for each sales call. Help them.

jective for each and every sales call, there is not much accomplished. I call this the "drive-through bakery/coffee shop" way to conduct sales meetings. Take a dozen donuts to your business meeting, talk about a lot of personal stuff, and nothing is really accomplished. Some "old school" sales professionals will tell you that this is part of starting or maintaining a great business relationship, but people are too busy today to worry about donuts! They have their bosses breathing down their necks and wanting to see results, not social gatherings.

> **Epilogue**
> *Your customers expect that their time will be used wisely.*

Conduct Account Reviews

Every customer/client needs to have an account profile. Why? This gives visibility and transparency into your key accounts from the top down in your organization. The profile needs to include general information about the

> **Assignment**
>
> Create a formal account review form with all relevant customer information. Review this information on a regular basis with your sales professionals on a weekly, monthly, and annual basis.

billing; key decision-makers at the company; pain points, including those that have been addressed along with potential ones; and the budget for all products and services. When this information is visible and available, you will be able to conduct account reviews on a regular and recurring basis.

Customer data needs to be reviewed on a regular basis with your sales professionals. This information is also useful for internal communications with key executives who regularly monitor sales performance. This is the detail that helps support the overall annual sales plan.

> **Epilogue**
> *The more your sales professionals know, the better they will be.*

51

Establish In-Depth Account/ Customer Visibility

Beyond a formal account review, customer information needs to be readily shared among the sales team and key executives. Whether you are a small company or a large organization, you have the capability to provide in-depth information on every account and customer. You can make a minimal investment in creat-

> ### *Assignment*
>
> Research and establish a methodology to provide in-depth account and customer information to your sales team and key executives. Then share the information with your sales professionals.

ing manual forms and reports, or you can research and invest in new sales force management technology that gives you the capability to share customer information through the Internet on a real-time basis. Transparency is the key. The more information collected and documented from your sales team, the more opportunities there will be to lead discussions on business strategy and direction.

> ### Epilogue
> *By sharing information, everybody is better off.*

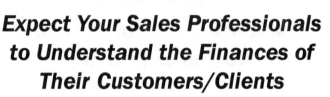

Expect Your Sales Professionals to Understand the Finances of Their Customers/Clients

Without a doubt, your sales professionals need to have business and financial acumen, regardless of whether your customers and clients are public or private compa-

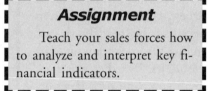

Assignment

Teach your sales forces how to analyze and interpret key financial indicators.

nies. Public company information is easier to obtain, but if you have a great relationship with customers who run a private company, then, because you are a trusted advisor, they should share financial information with you. This is a competency that, as a sales manager, you cannot live without. All your sales professionals need to understand the finances of their customers and clients. Understanding a customer's financial situation, income statement, balance sheet, and cash flow will be helpful for the sales professional's assessment of solving business problems, return on investment for products/services, and the customer's ability to pay.

The people drive the numbers and the numbers are the metrics for success and business sustainability. Additionally, customer bad credit and inability to pay create cash flow and financing problems.

Epilogue

Sales professionals who understand the numbers have a lot of credibility.

All Extra-Curricular Activities Must Involve a Sale

As the sales manager, it is your responsibility to explain to your senior executives the activities and budget expenses that get approved every month. No doubt this is not old news. If you want to ensure that your sales expenditures related to extra-curricular activities are justifiable,

> ### Assignment
>
> Explain to your sales team that extra-curricular activities with prospects/customers/clients must include a tie back to a sale. This sale needs to be documented as part of your existing business or your sales pipeline of opportunities.

make sure that all activities involve a customer focus. Every customer activity, including extra-curricular activities, needs to involve a business objective that involves a sale. If this is an existing customer, then the sales process might include an extension of work. If this is a new prospective customer, then the sales process will be concentrated on closing a deal.

Epilogue

Without being trite, this seems obvious. However, it makes a huge difference when your senior executives are asking you about the dollars you are spending to close deals.

54

Establish the "No Excuse" Rule

This is not just related to motivating your sales force. What is the "no excuse" rule? It's about setting the sales-leadership and cultural tone that mistakes will happen during the sales process, but individuals and all team members will take accountability for the ultimate outcomes of each and every interaction with pros-

> ### *Assignment*
>
> Make "no excuses" part of your normal coaching and performance reviews. As you review performance and conduct account reviews, make it a point to review the root causes of any failures.

pects/clients/customers. The majority of root causes, 87 percent in fact, are within the control of sales professionals and their prospects/customer/clients. Only about 13 percent are outside the sales professional's control.

The great 2006 Superbowl coach of the Indianapolis Colts, Tony Dungy, not only has "No Excuses" posted on a poster board in the locker room, but this is one of his five non-negotiables if you are going to be part of his team.

> ### Epilogue
>
> *Never, ever, let your sales professional make excuses for failures and/or not closing a deal.*

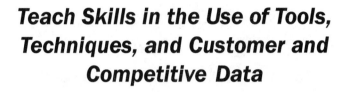

Teach Skills in the Use of Tools, Techniques, and Customer and Competitive Data

Sales management involves coaching your sales team. Great coaches teach the fundamentals of the game. In the game of sales there are tools, techniques, and information that help drive higher performance, knowledge, and

> **Assignment**
>
> Identify your sales tools, techniques in your sales process and information that is relevant to help your team close more deals.

better decision-making. These include but are not limited to: financial statements, budgets, business and sales plans, sales and business application technologies, sales models, training, learning technique, personal coaching, and customer and competitive information you can now find on the Internet (search Google, Yahoo finance, and other relevant business intelligence–gathering search tools).

> **Epilogue**
>
> *What separates the good sales managers from the great sales managers is the focus on teaching fundamental sales skills using business tools, techniques, and relevant sales information.*

56

Provide Opportunities for Mentoring and Sharing Lessons of Success With Customers/Clients

Top-notch sales professionals love to demonstrate successful sales behaviors. Why not leverage the skill, expertise, and successful sales behaviors demonstrated by your best performers? Mentoring is a cost-effective way to assign privilege that not all sales team members get to participate in. This creates

Assignment
Identify your top sales performers and ask who is willing to teach others on the team the sales behaviors that work for your organization. Assign top performers to teach/mentor others on the skills that work. Establish a formal mentoring process for your sales professionals.

internal competition for top performers to outperform other top performers and incentivizes mediocre performers to step up their game to model successful sales behaviors and techniques. That motivates top performers. The mentoring process and the privilege to share lessons of success raises the bar of performance for other team members. Raising the bar of performance through mentoring offers a unique privilege to those who can teach and share their knowledge with willing learners.

Mentoring accomplishes the important business objectives: fosters commitments to improve performance, takes advantage of existing knowledge and expertise, and distributes sales leader/manager coaching accountabilities. This can have a lasting performance impact on those who mentor and those who are mentored. The teacher becomes the student and the student can become the teacher. Learning becomes a self-managed process as part of your sales team culture.

> **Epilogue**
> *The internal drive and competitive nature of top-notch sales professionals to raise the bar on performance is a natural occurrence.*

57

Provide Coaching to Improve Performance and Strength

Have you ever worked for a manager who was a poor communicator, coach, and motivator? If you have had that experience, you know that it's non-inspiring and a downright waste of your time if you are a top sales performer and a high-potential professional. Your team will be motivated by your ability to provide expert coaching and performance feedback. Coaching is a skill and an art. Coaching is

> **Assignment**
> Invest some time to read the book *Quiet Strength*, by Tony Dungy (Tyndale, 2007), the coach of the Indianapolis Colts. In it, you'll find great ideas for improving your coaching skills, whether it's in football or sales. Great coaches are great coaches in anything they do.

different from the old model of being "the boss and you will do what I say or else." The skill and art of coaching is identifying what's expected of an individual to perform, then identifying his or her strengths, and matching sales professionals' strengths to their assignments—their customers, clients, products, and/or services/territories.

Lay out the fundamentals, be clear about competencies and accountabilities, and be sure your sales professionals are matched with their capabilities to reach their professional success. Sounds easy, but this is the most difficult job of a sales manager.

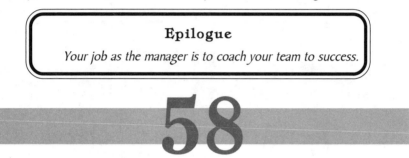

Epilogue

Your job as the manager is to coach your team to success.

58

Provide Ongoing Learning Opportunities to Improve Sales Proficiency

Both the book *The Extraordinary Leader*, by Zenger and Folkman, and the Design Group and Lominger competency model focus on a *key* skill that most managers do not do very well—provide

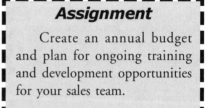

Assignment

Create an annual budget and plan for ongoing training and development opportunities for your sales team.

learning and development opportunities for those professionals who report to them. Having a dedicated focus on learning and developing your team's professional skills is a must in today's competitive marketplace. Think about this: If learning, developing new skills, and applying this to your current and potential customers can provide you with a competitive advantage, specifically because everyone else is providing lukewarm solutions to customers' business problems, then there is a way to separate yourself as a great sales manager. Providing ongoing learning to improve your sales proficiency is key to success. When budgets are tight or get cut, the first thing to go is the training or development budget. Don't do it, for the sake of your sales team. Sales professionals need to keep their skills sharp.

Do you want to have the sharpest competitive team in your industry? Then make this a priority, and don't relent on cutting budgets or not investing in your people. You will ultimately lose if you do.

Epilogue

If you don't incorporate training and development into your routine functions, and then continue to support training and learning for your sales team, your competition will.

Train and Have Your Top Sales Performers Conduct the Hiring of New Sales Recruits

As the sales manager, if you have been able to hire and retain "A" players and top sales performers, then you have a stable of top decision-makers. In addition to their ability to deliver results, there is the probability that they will want to continue in a culture that values collaboration and teamwork, and encourages sharing best practices. Leverage their ability to help you in the very important hiring process. One way to ensure that you will always hire the best sales professionals is to use a tested and proven process— the "Topgrade" approach. This process is well documented and has delivered top results for sales managers. In addition to hiring top sales performers, you also create a culture of top performance, and then your top sales performers will want to be part of the decision-making for new

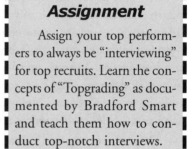

Assignment

Assign your top performers to always be "interviewing" for top recruits. Learn the concepts of "Topgrading" as documented by Bradford Smart and teach them how to conduct top-notch interviews.

hires. Top performers, though competitive, want to work with other top performers. Train them to conduct "Topgrade" interviews and collaborate on what they learn about new sales hires.

Epilogue
Your best hires will come from the recruiting and hiring process in which your top performers have bought into your performance philosophy and have applied the concepts of "Topgrading" hiring.

60

Role-Play Successful Sales Skills

Why do sports teams practice? The answer is obvious: Practice and preparation give you the capacity to deliver under pressure. There is no substitute. The more you practice great sales skills, the probability of your success increases to

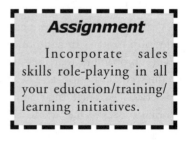

Assignment

Incorporate sales skills role-playing in all your education/training/ learning initiatives.

the point where you are confident in your ability to deliver the deal. You've played it out in your mind 100 times, and then it boils down to execution. Your body follows your mind when it comes to repetition. Competitive sales managers have a rule: rather than sending someone out on a sales call and "learning the hard way," create a working/training environment that expects that you will role-play to develop and enhance successful sales skills.

> ### Epilogue
> *There is no better way to learn about successful sales skills than in a simulated environment. That's the way great sports teams practice, practice, and practice.*

Train Sales Professionals in the "Language of Business"

The language of business is all about creating sustainable profits. Some might argue it's about creating wealth, but I would argue that wealth created without the ability to sustain a business for the long term is really investing. Sales professionals that are highly motivated want to in-

> **Assignment**
> Pick up and read *The Great Game of Business*, by Jack Stack (Bantam Doubleday Dell Publishing Group, Inc., 1994). Teach the concepts to your sales team.

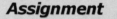

crease their wealth, especially for all their hard work. On the other hand, as an organization and sales manager, it's your job to align your team to the overall business goals of the organization and the understanding of the "language of the business." This provides the fundamental tool necessary to work within your organization and with your customers and clients. This also provides for a common platform of clear, effective, and direct communications within the company. The numbers of the company are the starting point.

> ### Epilogue
> *In addition to understanding the language of the sales process, all of your sales team members should be educated in the language of business—it's all about the numbers!*

Teach Sales Professionals to Uncover Pain, Budget, and Decision-Making With Their Customers/Clients

In my tenure as a sales professional, I've researched and distilled a sales process that gets to the core of any business transaction. Some people call these concepts fancy process names and include a lot of fluff, but at the end of the sales day, it really boils down to the

Assignment

Establish account reviews that require your sales professionals to describe and document customers' pain points, their budget to resolve the business problems, and who the key decision-makers are.

following key activities: uncovering pain points (what is the business problem that the customer/client is really trying to solve), budget (how much money are they willing to spend and/or invest in solving that business problem), and who is the decision-maker (who's going to sign the purchase order and/or statement of work).

Epilogue

This is the sales trilogy: pain, budget, and key decision-makers. Focus your sales attention on these three areas and you will be successful. Uncover this information and then capture it to make the sale.

63

Teach Sales Professionals Project Management Skills

There's a teaching tool of which I bet you haven't thought. I've read hundreds of books on sales, and not one talks about or teaches the necessity to focus skill in the area of great project management. Why do you want to teach your sales professionals project management skills? Managing an account/client is exactly like managing

Assignment

Learn and teach the concepts of project management to your sales professionals or enroll them in a quick course. Use the concepts as presented by the Project Management Institute, *A Guide to the Project Management Body of Knowledge* (Project Management, 2000). It'll pay for itself.

a project. Regardless of whether you are selling a product or service, it fits into a project.

Businesses manage by projects. This includes understanding the customer's processes, time, costs, quality, human resources, communications, risks, and procurement. This will facilitate and enhance external performance in front of your client and will also have internal benefits to your organization as your sales team will be functioning and communicating in a way that the business in question will understand.

Epilogue

It can be a huge competitive advantage when your sales professionals exhibit project management skills.

64

Teach Listening Skills

What??? Can you hear me now? Sounds familiar, right? I have coached and interviewed thousands of customers and clients, and I have uncovered a secret. The single most deficient sales competency is the skill

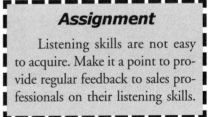

Assignment

Listening skills are not easy to acquire. Make it a point to provide regular feedback to sales professionals on their listening skills.

of listening. What did I say? Asking great questions and really probing and listening to the customer are skills that are necessary to differentiate *good* sales professionals from *great* ones. I would argue that when you have a highly motivated sales professional who uses the skills of great questioning and listening, that he or she will produce more revenue and demonstrate behaviors that are more closely tied to underlying motivational factors. This includes the drive to understand a customer's business problems and the willingness to associate his or her work to the likeness of the customers. Top sales professionals are motivated by the opportunity to be experts in verbal communications and presentations.

> **Epilogue**
>
> *Your best sales professionals have high levels of expertise in listening skills. Listening skills begin with an open mind, taking notes during a conversation, and clarifying what your customer is telling you.*

65

Teach High-Impact Consulting Skills

What are high-impact consulting skills? These are similar to project management skills as identified in Quick Idea #63. These include planning for a prospect call, account meeting, or customer interaction; building trust with your customer through quality work and leadership; communication skills for listening; verbal and written skills; and change

Assignment

Think about the last time you either hired or interacted with a top-notch sales professional. Did he or she exhibit high-impact consulting skills? Make this part of your overall competency learning set and teach your sales team to exhibit these types of skills.

management. I'd like to focus on the change management aspect of incorporating this into your sales management tool kit.

Change is tough for customers. If they have been working with a competitor, and you are moving into a new business relationship, then your sales professional will be motivated to create an environment that fosters the connection to this new business arrangement. Always keep change management at the top of your list when you are teaching all high-impact consulting skills to your sales professionals. If you want to demonstrate a competitive advantage, then teach your sales team to demonstrate high-impact consulting skills—for example, change management.

Epilogue

Most businesses today want solutions to their business problems, and this means they are looking for someone who can assist them beyond just selling a product or service.

Allow Time for Reading New Books and Articles on the Topic of Successful Selling

Sales professionals are highly motivated by investing time in learning. I've found that there is a correlation between the amount of time spent to really make more sense of new ideas and the world around, and overall success. I have found that there is a high probability well-read folks will be your most productive sales professionals. As the old adage says, "time is money," and everyone who understands that can be a successful sales professional. However, you must highly motivate sales performers to value learning as part of their career development and performance. Top performers make it a point to learn about new sales ideas, and how the competition is performing, and how to apply a new sales skill or technique.

Assignment

During your sales meetings, either assign a new book and/or article or have one of the people on your team share with the group an overview of a recent book or article.

Top-notch sales professionals never stop learning. It's part of their DNA. Motivate them informally and formally to include this behavior on a regular basis. You will see enhanced performance.

Epilogue

Learning is a life and career commitment.

Give Guidance on Qualifying Prospects

Your sales professionals are highly motivated to close the deal. However, I would offer that this motivational factor of closing the deal can sometimes override the skills necessary to thoroughly qualify all of your prospects. Because acquiring more clients is one of the strongest motivating factors for sales professionals, you must continually give guidance on the skills of listening, as mentioned in Quick Idea #64, and questioning, so that your sales professionals really understand how to solve a customer's business problem. Make no mistake—this is a huge investment of your time as a sales manager. But it's also imperative for you to define your

> ### *Assignment*
> Define your process of qualifying prospects. Communicate this to your sales team and hold them accountable for investing their time wisely with this process.

process when qualifying prospects. It first starts with a definition of a prospect. If you call on a prospect, you need to uncover pain, budget, and decision-makers, and then fit them into your defined sales pipeline. Your sales team will be highly motivated when they invest their time wisely and see the results of transforming well-qualified prospects into customers.

> ### Epilogue
> *Qualifying prospects is not about closing the deal. It's about uncovering real customer pain, budget, and decision-making to fix business problems.*

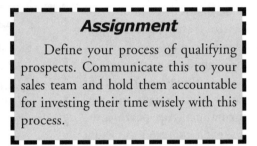

Use Failure as a Learning Tool

Here's a tip for all you sales managers from my mom (yes, my mom). These are life lessons that I think apply in today's competitive sales world. There are two types of failures: one is not taking the time to prepare and practice, and the second is over-preparing and trying too hard—yes, you can oversell the customer/client. In other words, you talk too much and don't listen enough, you assume too much about the deal and don't ask enough questions, or you bash your competition to the point where the customer thinks that, if you behave this way now, this is what they can expect to see if you conduct business together. Both types of failure offer sales lessons learned. However,

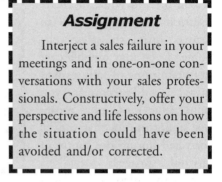

Assignment

Interject a sales failure in your meetings and in one-on-one conversations with your sales professionals. Constructively, offer your perspective and life lessons on how the situation could have been avoided and/or corrected.

the objective is that when you do fail (and you will), use it as an opportunity to learn about improvement in sales performance.

You don't have to beat up anyone about failure, because we all fail at some point during the sales cycle. The key, though, as the sales manager, is to use failure experiences as learning tools to improve.

Epilogue

Your top sales professionals are highly motivated to learn from failures. They will improve performance because they hate to lose.

69

Analyze Sales Mistakes as Lessons Learned

Sales mistakes are different from sales failures. Failures, as described in Quick Idea #68, are done deals when the game is over. Mistakes, on the other hand, are those opportunities when the game is still on and you can create solutions or change course to recover during the sales cycle. Some of you may quibble over my definitions of failures and mistakes, but I recommend you think about mistakes as proactive opportunities that can be corrected during the course of any sales process. Mistakes, during the sales process, will

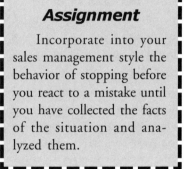

Assignment

Incorporate into your sales management style the behavior of stopping before you react to a mistake until you have collected the facts of the situation and analyzed them.

happen. Also, don't jump to conclusions about any mistakes during the sales process until you have collected all the facts. As a sales manager, it is imperative for the motivation of your sales professionals that you always collect the facts before you make any conclusions on a mistake. Fact-based analysis is the cornerstone of sales management, and will lead your team to an appreciation that you are being objective when mistakes are made.

Epilogue

You'll have no greater respect than what comes from your ability to analyze sales mistakes and collect all the facts before you react.

Teach How to Overcome Objections

Every sales book in the world (at least the ones that I've read) provides ideas, advice, and instructions on how to overcome objections in the sales process. They offer advice like what to say when a price is too low, what to say when they use the competition, and what to say when they're sorry but just not interested...say, say, say, say, say. As a sales manager, you've either been there yourself because you were in the sales trenches or else you've heard them all from the people you lead. "Sorry, not interested." "Not budgeted." "Price is too high." "We use the competition."

Assignment

Take out of your training all the lists of the 15 or so objections that you typically hear from a customer. Use this information only to redirect that natural sales tendency/behavior to say, say, say, respond, respond, respond with that of question, understand, solve business problem.

Here's the secret sauce on how to overcome sales objections: address them straight up with the customer when you uncover them. Although a great choreographed list of responses is good to know, the better approach is to confront and constructively address the objection by asking specific questions. Objections are a way of life in the sales profession. The way objections are handled greatly increases or decreases your likelihood of really understanding the objection and moving closer to closing a deal, thereby earning the trust of a prospect and/or customer. If you are prepared, teach your sales team how to respond, and you will increase their motivation and be ahead of your competition.

Epilogue

There is no way around the issue of receiving objections during the sales process. The key is how you respond to them.

71

Invite an Industry Pro to Give Advice and Coaching

Industry pros have a lot of intellectual property (IP) that they have gathered during their experiences and careers. I call this "a lot of sales scar tissue from the sales battles fought, won, and lost." There's such a wealth of information and opportunity to learn and grow from someone who has

> **Assignment**
>
> Find an industry pro who is willing to offer his or her perspectives on customers, the market, skills, and prospects. Assign that person to give advice and to coach during formal training or even in independent, one-on-one coaching with each of your sales professionals.

"been there and done that." Sales professionals have the unique motivational character to want to learn. So, leverage opportunities for "old pros" to share their wisdom and key learning. Whether the pro is in retirement or currently working, he or she can oftentimes bring into your organization different perspectives of which someone may not have thought.

Gain wisdom on success and take advice on "mistakes" before you and/or your team have to experience them firsthand. This truly makes a difference in motivation and performance. Transferring IP from those who have been in the sales trenches might give you and your team an opportunity to learn from mistakes, avoid mistakes, and, better yet, the ability to learn from their successes.

> ### Epilogue
> *Quality experience matters, and so does gaining wisdom from those who have "been there and done that."*

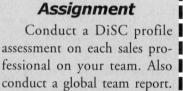

Conduct a DiSC Profile on Each Salesperson

The DiSC profile is a self-assessment tool that identifies common behaviors and preferences in communication styles. The DiSC profile is a validated instrument that identifies Dominance, Influence, Steadiness, and Conscientiousness. These are the four key attributes that are identified, defined, and un-

Assignment

Conduct a DiSC profile assessment on each sales professional on your team. Also conduct a global team report. More information about DiSC: *http://en.wikipedia.org/wiki/DISC_assessment*; and *www.internalchange.com/inscape*.

covered during the assessment process. More than two million people have taken the DiSC profile. Individuals and managers find the information useful, not just in understanding a common approach to their communication styles, but also to those of their customers and clients. The foundation of this instrument is the 1928 book by William Marston, *Emotions of Normal People*. The assessment only takes a few minutes to complete and is available electronically online.

> **Epilogue**
> *The use of DiSC as a self-assessment instrument is valid, with more than two million participants to date. This will give you insight into the behavior and communication styles of every person on your team.*

73

Share and Interpret DiSC Profile Results

Once you have conducted the DiSC profile assessments, it's imperative that you then do two things. First, have the results inter-

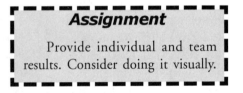

Assignment

Provide individual and team results. Consider doing it visually.

preted for clarity and understanding. Second, share the results with the individual respondents, and then collectively as a team. As a follow-up team exercise, make it visual. Make four large squares of tape on the floor, labeled D, i, S, and C. Then have your sales professionals stand in the appropriate square. Have them look around to see who has what style.

It makes a difference how communication styles can be varied to make the best results. Conducting assessments about style and/or performance is important. How you interpret and share the results of those assessments is even more important.

Epilogue

Invest the time to get professional guidance on DiSC profile assessment and results. This will enable you, as the sales manager, to offer constructive insights into valid and successful behaviors and communication styles with your sales staff.

74

Teach Your Sales Professionals to Use the DiSC With Their Customers/Clients

After you have assessed and interpreted the DiSC profile results, your next step is to use this information to evaluate the behavior and communication styles of the key decision-makers for your prospects and clients. This is not a perfect science in interpreting behaviors

Assignment

Incorporate DiSC training into your formal sales training routines. For more information on DiSC training see *Emotions of Normal People* by William Moulton Marston, PhD, 1928; Wikipedia; and Inscape Publishing at *www.inscapepublishing.com*. Also, include instructions on interpretations during your one-on-one coaching experiences or with your entire team.

and communication styles, but it does provide you with a framework to evaluate the key decision-makers. Encourage your sales professionals to really take notice, when they have the chance to observe and interact with key decision-makers at your prospects' and current customers' companies. Having this knowledge will facilitate better communications, and will foster a greater sense of how to respond to a prospect/customer, because this includes instructions on how to respond and react to the four primary emotional categories of behavioral responses.

Epilogue

A new skill in observing prospect and customer behavior and communication styles will be a great asset.

75

Send Your Sales Professionals to Professional Writing School

Writing for purpose and clarity are important fundamentals in the sales process. A sales professional who can write effectively essentially has the control in business discussions and negotiations. Why? During any written conversation or negotiations on a deal, the person who is documenting

---

Assignment

Benjamin Franklin, one of our founding fathers, a statesmen, and the ultimate sales profession (if you watch the History Channel) was a master at the pen and writing competency. Check out some of his quotes, which still have relevance today.

---

what is being discussed or negotiated is filtering what is being heard and translating that into written documentation with their own bias (for example, "this is what I heard but I am going to put it into my context based on my sales objectives"). This enables a quicker and more responsive process, to the ultimate conclusion of closing a deal with proposals, statements of work (SOWs), and contracts. Also, remember that your customers and clients perceive your sales competence based on your ability to write in a clear, concise, and effective manner.

Epilogue

Make an investment to train your sales professionals in the skill of written communication.

76

Send Your Sales Professionals to Professional Acting School

As a sales manager, why would I even consider sending my sales professionals to acting school? Acting skills teach the ability to memorize lines of speech

---

Assignment

Investigate the cost and implementation of professional acting classes for your sales professionals.

---

and respond to situations on the stage. The skills learned as part of professional acting (for example, being clear and concise, being articulate, and interpreting body language during a given scene) all apply to the skill and art of professional sales. This may seem a little odd, but the correlation to prospect/customer interactions is quite similar. If you have ever had the chance to videotape a sales call, you will see that the exchanges in communications of a sales professional and his/her client are very similar.

> ### Epilogue
>
> *Acting is a bit different from role-playing in formal sales curriculums. This opportunity offers an exploratory way beyond typical sales scripts to enhance performance and preparation for "on-stage" performances.*

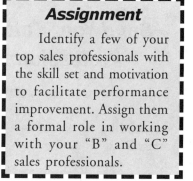

Establish a Mentoring Program

There is no better way to engage and motivate your top sales professionals with a passion for teaching than to establish a mentoring program. A mentoring program gives passionate performers the opportunity to share what they know and offer suggestions for performance improvement. A great mentor can provide advice in a way that is not perceived as threatening, that is not tied to compensation increases, and/or has no fear of reprisal. This can go a long way toward establishing constructive feedback about the sales initiatives you are trying to accomplish. It can also enhance performance and give leadership opportunities to those individuals who want to be included as part of your succession planning work.

Assignment

Identify a few of your top sales professionals with the skill set and motivation to facilitate performance improvement. Assign them a formal role in working with your "B" and "C" sales professionals.

A formal mentoring program has significant benefits. It helps identify and uncover top sales performers who have the skill and competence to coach, it creates a learning culture that transcends the boss, and it provides opportunities for those aspiring to become a sales manager.

> **Epilogue**
> *Those who can, do...and teach!*

78

Provide Constructive Feedback About Negative Behavior

As the sales manager, tolerance of negative behavior is non-negotiable and unacceptable. There are two potential impacts of negative behavior: negative behavior rubs off on other coworkers who

> ### *Assignment*
>
> Make a commitment to not let negative behavior go unaddressed, even though it's sometimes easier to take the path of least resistance. It's never fun to reprimand, but it comes with the territory as a sales manager.

are susceptible to being influenced, and negative behavior that is not addressed by the manager has the potential of becoming common practice. If the behavior becomes common practice and the manager does not address it in a constructive way, your top performers will question your competence and capabilities as their sales manager.

When you observe negative behavior by anyone on your sales team, the behavior needs to be addressed immediately, and preferably in a private discussion about the behavior in question. Your credibility as a sales manager will be tested. One test is how you respond to negative behavior on the job. If you don't address negative sales behaviors, your credibility will be put into question. Repetitious, ongoing negative sales behaviors that do not get addressed are a sure way not only to lose credibility as a manager, but also to get fired. Be a leader.

Epilogue

Save your credibility by addressing negative behavior quickly and effectively.

79

Establish Yourself as the Coach

Great sales leaders are great coaches. Do you want to motivate your sales team? Then be a great coach and not just a manager. Great managers/coaches take accountability for the teaching aspects of their job and constructively help their sales professionals become top performers. Sales managers who focus on coaching win high praise from their teams and contributors. Why? Because they win, and set expectations to win and be held accountable for results. This is how to fulfill the drives that motivate sales professionals. Sales managers can also become mentors for high performers. Their inspiration and

Assignment

Pick up as many books you can about winning coaches. Based on your self-proclaimed style of sales management, incorporate what you learn and apply an aspect of coaching in your sales management style.

candid constructive feedback will always be well received and welcome. "A" players want to continually improve, and they look to the coach of the sales team to provide this type of leadership. "B" and "C" players see the success that happens when you apply great coaching to your team. If they have the drive, they will take your lead as a great sales coach. Deep down, everyone wants to succeed. Be an active coach: focus on people's strengths and help them achieve top-level performance.

Epilogue

Players need coaches—people who will push them into higher performance. Have you been an active coach or a critic?

Create "Real Life" Sales Learning Opportunities and Teach the Lessons Learned

Many professions create "real life" situations in a controlled environment to practice skills and teach how to improve performance. My dad was a professional fireman and captain of his fire team. They would set up practice situations with real burning houses, and he would direct and lead his team on fire protection, life-saving operations, and team communications. There's nothing like being in a burning house and having to put out a fire, save a life, and be accountable for your team members to return safely with a job accomplished. When you are in the line of fire during a sales call, I hope you have practiced for it. Setting up "real life" sales experiences before you enter the line of fire that your sales team will encounter will give you a better opportunity for success and take some of the risk out of the sales equation. Use these as teaching opportunities.

Teach your sales team that risks are a part of their day-to-day lives and that preparation is the key. Also use lessons learned from failure to help make better decisions as you look at new sales opportunities. Better practicing on the practice field than in front of a customer and client and not know what to do or what's expected of you.

Assignment

Develop a method to create "real life" sales learning opportunities for your sales team. Spend time to document the facts of the situation. Use this information as a teaching tool—not as a "hammer", but to illustrate what happens in real life, in the life of a sales professional.

Epilogue
Success is what happens when you prepare for failure.

81

Develop a Method to Transfer Sales "Knowledge"

A huge key in sustainable sales consistency is the ability to capture and transfer sales knowledge. The type of knowledge to which I am referring includes accounts, pipeline of opportunities, skills and competencies, and everything else you can get your hands on about your business and industry. We call it *competitive intelligence*. All of this information is very valuable. It's a must in today's competitive environment to capture and develop a method for transferring this sales knowledge and making it a part of your DNA. Communication of this knowledge is vital for business continuity so that you will not be held responsible for knowledge walking out the door if someone leaves your organization.

Epilogue

The knowledge age is here. We rely on critical information to conduct our business. Sales knowledge is a valuable commodity. The more you have, retain, and transfer, the more you reduce the risk of sales knowledge walking out the door.

Spend Time Developing Yourself as the Sales Leader

Based on thousands of sales leadership 360 assessments that I have touched through the years, I have found that the second-most critical competency gap for managers is developing yourself as a leader. You may have been promoted because you were a great contributor and an "A" player sales professional. I can't emphasize enough that your team watches your behavior. Are you a learner? If not, you ought to be. Sales leadership

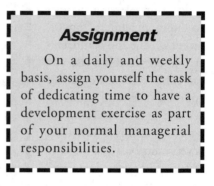

Assignment

On a daily and weekly basis, assign yourself the task of dedicating time to have a development exercise as part of your normal managerial responsibilities.

skills are the keys to motivating your sales team. Do you have the understanding and willingness to develop yourself as a manager? It is a wise manager who invests the time to read about and keep up to speed on the trends in one's given industry. It's also important to develop a practice of dedicating the time and energy to develop new thoughts and ideas outside the constraints of common sales practices.

When you do invest the time to develop yourself, it is reflected in your leadership skills. Your sales team will observe that development and come to understand that it is a priority. When you demonstrate this behavior, your team will take notice and begin to understand how important self-development is, especially with you taking the lead.

Epilogue
The student is the teacher and the teacher is the student. There is wealth invested as a direct result of investing in you!

83

Understand and Teach the Key Metrics of the Business

Nothing is more important than understanding the game of business as it relates to the key metrics of how the business runs and what is measured. This is a critical competency that signifies your overall business understanding. How you teach the numbers of the business will directly impact the performance of your sales team members, and will also have an affect on your overall sales results. The income statement, balance sheet, cash flows, and P&L will all contribute to your managerial capability and leadership for your sales team. The information, and the ability to understand and interpret it, is critical to making key decisions about adjustments that are proactively necessary as part of your sales execution on a regular and recurring basis. As the sales manager, understand,

---

Assignment

Assign your team to read and understand your income statement, balance sheet, cash flow, P&L, and budget worksheets. There are *great books* out there that break these topics down in a way all can understand. Some of these books include: *Financial Intelligence* by Karen Berman and Joe Knight (Harvard Business School Press, 2006), *The Little Black Book of Budgets and Forecasts* by Michael C. Thomsett (American Management Association, 1988), *The Portable MBA in Entrepreneurship* by William D. Bygrave and Andrew Zacharakis (John Wiley & Sons, Inc., 2004) and *The ROI of Human Capital* by Jac Fitz-enz (American Management Association, 2000).

---

and teach what numbers are driving the business and how you as the sales team are going to positively impact the revenue, profit, and cost savings.

Epilogue

Business is all about the numbers. Top-notch sales professionals understand this.

84

Do Not Make an Investment in Sales Training Unless You Understand Individual and Team Competencies

Earlier in the book, I recommended you invest and implement a sales competency model. Why is it important to start with a competency model, and then make decisions associated with sales training? Well, the next time you walk into

Assignment

After you have selected a competency model (such as those available at *www.lominger.com* or *www.devinegroup.com*), define and assess competencies necessary for success in the job.

a budget discussion with your boss to fund sales training, he or she ought to ask what type of return on investment you will achieve, and the probability that you increase your revenue and profitability when you invest in sales training. Most sales managers think that sales training is the answer to individual and team performance.

This is a waste of money. Why? Sales training cannot be conducted until sales competencies and skills are defined for the job. Competencies are the foundation of identifying what's expected in the job and how the individual will be assessed for success. This will also give you an idea of identified competency gaps that will need to be addressed as part of your targeted sales training plan and investment to close the gaps and increase revenue.

Never, ever invest in sales training unless you have defined, assessed, and analyzed skills gaps so that the training you conduct is directly correlated to closing thoseskills gaps and identifying individual and team strengths in order to enhance overall performance. Training in the *hopes* of getting results (instead of seeing results) is what you will get if you do not follow this recommendation.

> **Epilogue**
> *Senior executives want tangible results, and want the business case to support an investment—even sales training.*

Teach Your Sales Professionals the Skill of Self-Performance Evaluation

Top sales performers evaluate their performance according to their goals and objectives. Motivation for sales professionals comes from two sources: self-evaluation, so that they can accomplish their goals and objectives, and from you as their sales manager. This is in addition to coaching, feedback, and support that your sales team receives from you. The skill of self-evaluation with regard to performance is what top professionals use as measuring sticks for their performance and success in accomplishing their sales goals. Typically, top sales professionals conduct self-

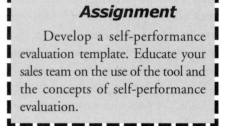

Assignment

Develop a self-performance evaluation template. Educate your sales team on the use of the tool and the concepts of self-performance evaluation.

performance evaluations on a regular and consistent basis. Teaching this skill of self-performance evaluation gives the sales manager another important tool in motivating and enhancing individual and team performance.

Epilogue

Self-performance evaluations are valuable feedback and motivation tools. Once the skill is developed to compare performance to established goals, this process becomes a powerful motivational tool.

Don't Waste Your Time With Trendy Training Fads

Every CEO, CFO, and COO I've advised and been associated with always asks about return on investment for training—including sales training. Their question is: if we are going to invest in training our sales team, how will this change performance to obtain addition revenue and increase profitability?

When an external sales trainer calls on you, or you have the urge to invest in sales training in order to change performance—STOP. Don't do it. Think about the importance of having defined sales competencies and understanding the gaps in those

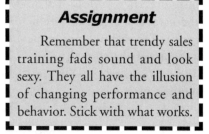

Assignment

Remember that trendy sales training fads sound and look sexy. They all have the illusion of changing performance and behavior. Stick with what works.

competencies so you can target your investments and have a higher probability and likelihood of a successful training investment. Reprogram yourself to first ask whether you have done a thorough job in defining and assessing sales competencies.

Epilogue

Training is only as good as the job you did as the sales manager doing upfront work on the competencies and skills necessary to be successful as a sales professional.

Your Intelligence Is Equal to the Thoroughness of Your Questions

What does this have to do with motivating your sales team? High performers understand that their motivation is contingent on their capabilities and skills. A huge myth is that the number-one skill that a sales professional needs to have is the ability to talk, talk, talk, talk, and talk. On the contrary; the skill and ability to ask in-depth business questions and uncover customer pain points puts the sales professional in the category of being intelligent and thoughtful, not in the category of the smooth talker. Top performers relish the opportunities to uncover and solve complex business problems. Sales professionals, although mostly good communicators and presenters, have not tapped the skill and art of effective questioning. The perception of intelligence does not solely come from a great Microsoft PowerPoint presentation.

> **Assignment**
>
> Establish the skill and art of asking thoughtful business questions as part of your regular sales coaching routine. Take time to observe this skill during your internal meetings and to evaluate this skill during sales calls.

Epilogue

The evaluation of intelligence comes from the thoroughness and thoughtfulness of the questions that are exchanged during any customer interaction.

88

Teach the Sales Team How to Use Sales Data

Quantitative information drives business, operations, and sales. All sales data should be part of your regular dialogue with your sales

---

Assignment

If you do not have established sales reports and reporting, make establishing a method to share the information a priority. Also, identify your methods of reporting critical sales data. Ensure that this information is shared with your sales team in daily, weekly, monthly, and annual meetings and conference calls.

---

team. They should have a clear understanding of the numbers that drive your business and your customers' business. There is great pride and motivation in taking the time to really understand what is driving a business—fixing problems, understanding and enabling growth, or trying to enhance overall performance. Lack of data makes it difficult to adjust sales team direction. Making decisions about aligning your sales team to meet their goals and objectives revolves around your ability to access and share critical sales data and business information.

Epilogue
Quantitative sales data is king!

89

Encourage Your Sales Team to Deliver Value on Each and Every Sales Call

Customers today don't have time for idle chit chat, donuts, and meals. Those days of sales calls are over. In today's competitive business environment, customers are looking for and wanting something of value from your sales professionals on each and every sales

Assignment

Establish a defined "value proposition" for your business, products, and services. Test this information with your existing clients and ask them what and how they made their decision to work with you or anyone on your sales team. Incorporate this feedback into your value proposition and ensure that your sales team is schooled in the ability to deliver this information on each and every sales call.

call. This includes, but is not limited to: thoughtful questions that provoke respectful challenges in thought processes, information and ideas that will assist in solving business problems, an understanding of your competitive differentiation and the value you bring to the relationship, and business case information that is helpful for them to evaluate whether or not to conduct business with you.

Epilogue

Relationships do matter. Value matters more in today's competitive business environment. Mix these two qualities together and you have a recipe for your sales team to succeed and your customers/clients to benefit as well. This is a true win-win situation.

90

Have the Right Systems and Processes in Place to Enable Maximum Productivity

Sales professionals understand that processes and systems enable sales execution. Processes that detail tasks and sales activities allow for the opportunity to enhance productivity and sustain levels of consistent sales delivery. Defined sales processes also communi-

cate to your organization that the sales execution expected from your sales team is aligned to your business strategy and key priorities. Having a sales system allows you to capture critical sales data in one technology platform. The integration of sales data with business operations and finance is critical to budgeting, planning, and day-to-day operations.

If you have processes defined, then establish a validation schedule so that your processes are reviewed on a regular and recurring basis for process improvement. With regards to sales systems, if you do have one, then begin the evaluation of a system that is cost effective and user-friendly. For those with existing sales systems, establish a process to review costs and enhance functionality while your business and customer base changes. A sales system enables and enhances sales productivity. Top sales performers understand that flawless execution and having the tools that enable the process combine for maximum productivity and translate into motivation to excel.

Epilogue

Defined sales processes facilitate consistency in sales execution and delivery.

91

Ring the Bell When Someone Makes a Sale

Ding dong! Whether you use a real bell or an e-mail, celebrate when someone makes a sale. This process creates a sense of accomplishment, pride, and enthusiasm for your sales team. You will also get visibility within your organization as your sales team

Assignment

Establish a formal process to "ring the bell" when you close sales. Whether you are in the office or you manage a virtual sales force, find a way to share the success of closing deals.

obtains this type of feedback on their performance to close sales. Some may argue that there is a diminishing return on motivation for your sales professionals. On the contrary. This process cannot be overused and/or or lose its value. Sales professionals love to see how their performance is making an impact for the organization, including meeting their goals and objectives.

Epilogue

Communicating and celebrating the sales closures never gets old.

Eliminate, as Much as Possible, the Tactical Sales Work

Although some administrative sales work is important, do not place emphasis on this type of work or any other work that does not add value. Sales professionals understand where their value is: closing deals and solving customers' problems. Motivation of your sales team will come from eliminating the tasks that do not add value and focusing on what doese. It can be a demotivator for top-notch sales professionals if there is too much emphasis on administrative/tactical sales work.

Assignment

Define what tactical work is a priority and ensure that this work gets done. Eliminate or delegate unnecessary tactical sales work. Determine if you need an inside sales administrator or to invest in a sales system to handle the administrative/tactical sales work.

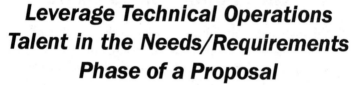

Epilogue

Sales professionals are focused on adding value. Value is defined as closing deals and solving customers' business problems. As the sales manager, if you place too much emphasis on the non-value added administrative/tactical sales work, then you will demotivate *your sales force.*

93

Leverage Technical Operations Talent in the Needs/Requirements Phase of a Proposal

Sales professionals want to create a customer/client proposal that blows away the competition and impresses the customer. Top-notch sales professionals understand that proposals include both "filling a rat hole" and solving a specific customer problem. They also understand that the complexity of today's proposals involves internal expertise in technical operations that assists in solving customer business problems. This also engages your internal operations team in the sales process, which gives them advanced notice to prepare to execute for the sales team if they win the proposal.

Assignment

Meet with your sales team and operation team. Set the expectation that, during the proposal stage of the sales cycle, the team is to decide on the inclusion of subject matter expertise in your operations. Also, set the expectation with your operations talent that they are to be involved in the proposal process if called upon by any of your sales professionals.

> ### Epilogue
> *Leveraging internal subject matter expertise, when appropriate, gives you the best chance to produce top-notch sales proposals and deals.*

94

Pilot New Sales Concepts When Given the Opportunity

Sales professionals learn by doing. They like to test different skills, techniques, and solutions to business problems. Encourage your sales team members to take their sales ideas and concepts and test them with your best customers. New concepts give a fresh perspective, and observing and measuring their success are huge motivators for sales professionals. Piloting new sales concepts gives you the opportunity to test changes in the sales process. You receive incremental feedback about the success and/or failure of the

Assignment

Identify a few new sales concepts from your sales team. Assign these new concepts to your top sales professionals and have them test the concepts with your best customers. Ensure that your customers understand that this is a pilot. Measure the success/failure. Apply what you learn to your overall sales approach.

new sales concepts. Sales professionals like to see success and eliminate risks/failures. When a pilot is successful and your sales professionals see that it works, include it in your overall sales process.

Epilogue

Sales professionals like to test different ideas and are eager learners. Take advantage of this natural instinct and you will motivate your sales staff.

Use a Sales Administration Technology

Invest in technology that will enable your sales team to leverage its focus on strategic sales activities while eliminating the administrative burden of reporting them. The technology should include, but not be limited to: prospecting, managing a sales funnel, customer information and contacts, invoicing, and closing deals. Reporting using sales administration technology can both greatly enhance the productivity of your sales team and provide the manager with critical information that can be readily available, without having to generate sales reporting information manually.

Assignment

Once an investment is made in a sales automation tool (such as the one available at *www.salesforce.com)*, define the business requirements for the inputs and outputs of the critical sales information that needs to be reported. That way you can match the correct sales tool with your needs.

Epilogue

Your sales tools will allow the sales manager to report on sales performance, provide coaching on performance enhancements, and be proactive in addressing changes in market conditions, with both your sales and your management teams.

96

Begin With the End in Mind When Giving Presentations

Your clients and customers have limited time. They want you to get to the point. This includes how you are going to solve their business problems and how much it's going to cost them. So when you are presenting the opportunity to talk about

Assignment

Teach your sales professionals that, when giving presentations, they should start with the end in mind. The end is the solution to a business problem that your customers are experiencing. This will teach your sales professionals to keep focused on solving business problems and ultimately closing more deals.

how you are going to solve a customer's business problem and/or offer a service/product, start with explaining what the end result is expected to be. Everyone is challenged with time constraints. If you teach your sales professionals to get to the point, your customers/clients will appreciate them more. They will see value that your competition does not deliver. They will also see a refreshing approach to their typical sales experience. This will close more deals, and, in return, motivate more of your sales force.

119

Epilogue

If you want to close more deals, which is the ultimate in sales motivation, then present your service/products/solutions with the end in mind.

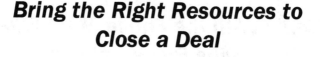

Bring the Right Resources to Close a Deal

Nothing is worse than bringing an entire group of unnecessary coworkers to a sales meeting when closing a deal. Top-notch sales professionals know how to coordinate and orchestrate the methods to close the deal. Ensure that during your discussions about closing the deal you have a detailed con-

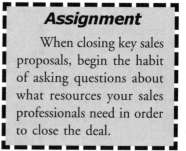

Assignment

When closing key sales proposals, begin the habit of asking questions about what resources your sales professionals need in order to close the deal.

versation on who in your organization needs to be included. Your sales professionals will have a good understanding of your customer/client preference for who needs to be included.

Be open, however, to the perspective that sometimes your sales professionals may need a little help from additional resources to close the deal. Top sales professionals know that the resource they need in order to close the deal is the most important aspect of the sales cycle. Support for their decisions when they need assistance is key to their motivation to close more deals and be successful.

> ## Epilogue
> *In most cases, err on the side that less is more. Most times, your sales professionals can close the deal.*

Survey Your Customers and Provide Constructive Feedback to Your Team

A formal approach to collecting information on the customer experience can provide constructive feedback on what you are doing well, what you can improve as part of the customer experience, and how to protect yourself from your competition—when you are open and transparent with the feedback from your best

> ### Assignment
> Develop a formal performance survey and administer it to the top 20 percent of your customer base. Analyze and dissect the information to determine gaps in performance and lessons learned as part of your customer partnerships. Share this information with your sales team to guide and direct performance improvement.

customers. Customers love to share their thoughts on how the business relationship can improve. Most customers who value the relationship will be open to sharing information on the contact they have with your team and your organization. Your sales team will also get the message that collecting the customers' feedback in a formal way will set the expectation that this information will be used in evaluating performance on an ongoing basis. It will also be the benchmark for relationship and process improvement, both of which are core competencies that your sales team needs to exhibit on a regular and recurring basis.

Epilogue

Formal surveying of customers show them that you value their opinions of the performance of your sales team.

Practice the Art of Outstanding Presentations

Quality is the name of the game. The first objective is to determine who is going to be included in the presentation. What skill sets and expertise are going to be necessary to deliver the key messages? The second step is understanding the objective of the presentation. Is this an educational exercise or a decision-making presentation? The third objective is to size up the participants—are these key executives and decision-makers, or mid-level managers and support people? How do they like to see their information? People are different and like to see information in different ways. Some want to see information graphically, whereas others prefer their information in a written format. This needs to be determined in order to anticipate the successful outcome of all outstanding presentations.

> ### *Assignment*
>
> Review the existing presentations that you deliver to your customers. Ask the following questions of your sales team: Do we have a clear value proposition for our products and services? Are the benefits to the customer clear and defined? Do we have a compelling business case that we offer our customers? What are the qualitative and quantitative metrics that drive value for our customers' business as we know it today, tomorrow and into the future?

Top-notch sales professionals expect to work for companies that are clear and have compelling reasons by which to build short and long term business relationships and customer value. Your sales team will be highly motivated when they think, feel and experience the alignment of your products and services when they can present a compelling business case that helps solve customers' business problems that provide outstanding customer value.

> ### Epilogue
>
> *All presentations need to be consistent with your organizational value proposition and employer brand.*

100

Establish and Maintain a Sales Funnel for Prospects and Deals

Regardless of the nomenclature, a sales funnel is just that—a funnel of a large number of prospects and existing business that gets narrowed down from the least likely prospects/deals to be signed to the most likely prospects/deals to be signed. The process is such that key questions are asked and answered while a prospect and/or deal gets closer to a close. What are the pain points of the cus-

Assignment

Establish a formal process to manage and monitor your sales funnel of activities. Report on your progress with your sales and management teams. Reporting this type of activity will keep your sales team focused on the priorities of closing deals as prospects move through your processes.

tomer? How much money/budget does the customer have to buy the product and/or service? And who are the key decision-makers regarding buying your product and/or service?

Additionally, you should assign a probability to each prospect's deal...for example, 75 percent, 50 percent, or 25 percent.

This will ensure that, in addition to the qualitative information you have on a prospect while they move through the sales funnel, you have been able to capture the likelihood of closing the deal.

Epilogue

As your sales professionals see their progress in moving prospects through the sales funnel to deal closure, they will be engaged and motivated to see the deal from inception to closure.

101

Ask a Lot of Status Questions for Any Prospective Deal

As the sales manager, it is your responsibility to understand the status of any key prospective deal. But make no mistake: This does not mean micromanaging every deal. Top-notch sales professionals take a lot of pride in their ability to manage their portfolio of deals they have to close. Asking questions about key deals, however, gives you the visibility you need in order to understand aligning appropriate resources in order to close as many deals as possible. This is not to be considered something that needs to be. Your job as the sales manager is to coach, improve performance, and close more deals. The only way you can accomplish this is by having a keen sense of awareness and applying the important skill of asking great questions about your prospective deals.

Assignment

Make it a point to "eat your own dog food." Ask constructive and thoughtful questions about all of your prospective deals.

Epilogue

A sales manager who doesn't ask thoughtful questions in order to understand the details and nuances of prospective deals is blind to what is going on.

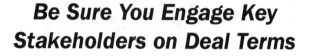

102

Be Sure You Engage Key Stakeholders on Deal Terms

Once you have a clear line of sight into the information that is collected by the sales professionals on any prospect and/or deal, ask the appropriate questions for clarity and understanding. Then, the next step is to be sure you engage and set expectations for

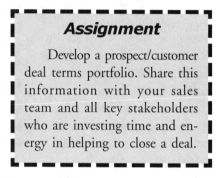

Assignment

Develop a prospect/customer deal terms portfolio. Share this information with your sales team and all key stakeholders who are investing time and energy in helping to close a deal.

resource alignment with your key internal stakeholders on deal terms to close a deal.

As you develop a track record of closing more deals, your sales team will experience a greater motivation to engage with internal subject-matter experts to increase their likelihood of closing as many deals as they can. This ends up being a win-win for the sales professional and for increasing your top-line results.

Epilogue

Proper coordination and collaboration with your sales team and key stakeholders greatly enhances your probability of closing more deals.

126

103

Solicit Internal Feedback on the Sales Process From Key Internal Stakeholders

In addition to collecting and evaluating feedback from your sales staff and customers, it would be wise to also proactively seek out feedback on the internal perceptions of how your sales process and your sales team are performing. Your sales team interacts with operations, finance, accounting, engineering, customer service, and so on. Key stakehold-

> ### Assignment
>
> Develop a methodology to collect formal and informal feedback on the performance of your overall sales process. Walk around. Ask key questions about internal stakeholders' experiences in working with your sales team. Document the information and act on it accordingly.

ers within the organization have a stake in the overall performance of your sales process. Conducted in a proactive and positive way, soliciting feedback will give you insights into opportunities to improve your overall performance and assist in locating underlying opportunities to motivate key sales team members.

As you collect and analyze the feedback, put it into constructive opportunities for process improvement. Share the information with your sales team. Obtain their thoughts on the opportunities and assign accountability to take action on process improvement. Top-notch sales professionals are always seeking opportunities for a "new way" of becoming more efficient, effective, and productive. The result: highly motivated sales team members who will close more deals! Wow, this is secret sauce.

> **Epilogue**
> *Proactively make solicitation of feedback about your sales process from your key internal stakeholders a regular occurrence.*

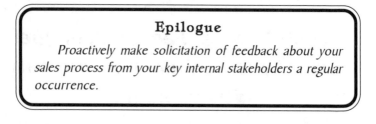

104

Deal With and Uncover All Facts Related to Any Deal

In any sales process and any sales deal, there are facts about the deal, and agendas that people bring based on their personal objectives. It is a must to separate fact from fiction with any deal. It is highly motivating when, as a sales professional, you learn the art and science of asking effective questions of your customer during the sales process.

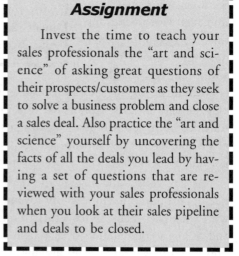

Assignment

Invest the time to teach your sales professionals the "art and science" of asking great questions of their prospects/customers as they seek to solve a business problem and close a sales deal. Also practice the "art and science" yourself by uncovering the facts of all the deals you lead by having a set of questions that are reviewed with your sales professionals when you look at their sales pipeline and deals to be closed.

Rather than rushing into closing a deal, invest the time necessary to really understand what problem your customer is trying to solve and the value that solving the problem creates for the customer. Teach your sales professionals to slow down, to ask a lot of questions about the potential deal, and to formulate a response to solve the problem by uncovering the facts of the customer's situation. There is nothing worse, from a sales professional's perspective than when a sales manager inserts himself or herself into the sales process and doesn't uncover and understand the facts of solving the customer's problem and getting to close.

Epilogue

In all sales processes and deal closures, there are a number of facts related to solving a customer's problem and closing a deal. Warning: If you do not invest the time necessary to really understand how you are solving the customer's problem by uncovering all the facts, you will be dealing in fiction and "hope" that you can close a deal.

105

Avoid Requests for Proposals (RFPs)

Avoid, if at all possible, responding to requests for proposals. There are good business reasons to heed this advice. The primary purpose of customers using RFPs is to set a baseline for negotiating the price of your products/services. Although it is a standard method of procurement, you do have a choice whether or not to participate in an RFP for your products and services. Typically, there are huge investments of the organization's and sales team's efforts to properly respond to RFPs. This does take away valuable sales time when you are administering and delegating RFP responses to your sales team. Although it's easy to uncover opportunities to respond to RFPs, frankly, it's a hell of a lot of work. My advice is to pick and choose which RFPs

> ### Assignment
>
> Assess your current process to respond to RFPs for your products and services. Determine the number of RFP wins, and the time allocation for your sales team to respond to RFPs, and do the math to determine the business value and profitability of responding to them.

to respond to, if you so decide. However, the amount of time necessary to respond may not be in the best interests of your profit margins and allocation of sales force time. If your sales team is incentivized by revenue and profitability, then they may push back and re-allocate their time to uncover business that is built on existing customer relationships and high-probability prospects.

> ### Epilogue
>
> *Nothing is more demotivating than for your sales team to invest a lot of time, energy, and effort, only to lose the RFP, especially knowing that the ultimate objective of an RFP is to negotiate your price.*

106

Help Find the Decision-Maker(s)

Right, wrong, or indifferent, your sales transactions are complicated—for one very important reason: finding the person/decision-maker who is the one who will make the call to do or continue doing business with you. The bottom line: You need to know who is on point with your customer to actually sign the purchase order, and who owns the budget to make the deal happen. It's a great opportunity as a sales manager to help

Assignment

Remember to coach your sales professionals on identifying and keeping track of the decision-makers for your products and services.

coach your sales professionals on this Quick Idea. The coaching that is imperative is that of asking questions about the key stakeholders during a sales transaction. You will uncover that there may be a lot of customer employees engaged in the sales cycle. But it's the identification of the key decision-maker that makes all the difference. As the manager, it's imperative that you coach your sales professionals on this skill in finding and knowing who the "real" decision-makers are—those who have the authority and ability to sign a purchase order.

Epilogue

Sales professionals can waste a lot of time building relationships and not uncovering the people who can really make a decision on a sales transaction.

107

Don't Expect Too Much Out of Trade Show Sales

Here's an investment that takes a lot of work, is expensive, and leaves your executive team wondering why you attend because it is difficult to determine a return on your investment (ROI). On the other hand, if you have no choice but to attend a trade show to sustain your brand among your competitors, then invest the time to plan and orchestrate how you expect your sales professionals to participate.

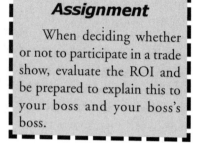

Assignment

When deciding whether or not to participate in a trade show, evaluate the ROI and be prepared to explain this to your boss and your boss's boss.

Make it an opportunity to acquire as many business cards as you can, allow time for your team to interact (not sell) with very interested prospects so they get to know each other, and use this as an opportunity to defend yourself against your competition, specifically educating interested prospects on your compelling value proposition. It's also a great time to do a little intelligence-gathering.

Based on years of experience working trade shows, I do question the return on investment in participating. Many organizations send their employees to trade shows, but rarely do decision-makers attend. They are too busy. That's worth noting.

Epilogue

Be sure that, when you decide to participate in a trade show, you understand that the expectation of obtaining a full pipeline of future prospects needs to be tempered.

108

Use Social Networks to Extend Opportunities With New Prospects

There are a number of online social networks to tap into in order to extend your brand and number of new prospects. LinkedIn,

Facebook, MySpace, Twitter, and so on, all have huge untapped potential for identifying and collaborating with new prospects. When you incorporate social networking into your customer space, it can provide some very powerful sales outcomes. It can provide another channel for

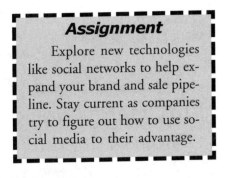

Assignment

Explore new technologies like social networks to help expand your brand and sale pipeline. Stay current as companies try to figure out how to use social media to their advantage.

your sales professionals to acquire more information about their clients/customers and the competition. It also has a unique and weird bonding experience for the younger generation not only to connect to your company but also to your sales professionals. This also has the potential social networking for lead generation. This has high potential and is now welcomed as a quicker and more efficient way for sales professionals to build their pipeline of prospective customers.

Epilogue

Compressing time and being more effective and efficient are always on the minds of your top sales professionals. Keep on top of the technology revolution and allow your sales professionals to do so as well.

109

Use Blogging Technology to Create a Brand Following and "Thought Leader" Position in Your Marketplace

In addition to social networks as mentioned in Quick Idea #108, you also have the opportunity to use another online means of leveraging the great work that your sales team delivers. Blogging technology allows an individual and/or an organization to submit thoughts, ideas, and opinions about a certain topic, and also allows a community of online users to provide feedback and their own thoughts, ideas, and opinions. Sales professionals who understand today's technology understand the power of connecting through these types of online interactions. You can create brand awareness, offer thought leadership from you and your sales team, and offer your compelling value proposition—all as means to create channels to the market that provide invaluable market intelligence you can then share with your sales team in a "real time" way. Remember that the drive to acquire information is a key motivator for sales professionals.

Assignment

Investigate and learn about the use of blogging technology. Meet with your Information Technology professionals and build a plan to use this technology for sales purposes. It's powerful and can provide you a competitive advantage. Your sales team will see the advantages when their sales pipeline becomes larger than they can handle. Now that's motivating.

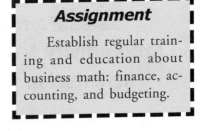

Epilogue

Don't underestimate the use of blogging technology.

110

Monetize Everything

This is the "holy grail." Your sales professionals are trained and educated about how to monetize every sales transaction. Pricing and terms of the deal are very important. Every sales transaction comes with an attached investment

Assignment

Establish regular training and education about business math: finance, accounting, and budgeting.

and/or expenditure. It's imperative that you teach your sales professionals to understand the opportunity to not only acquire and close deals, but also really understand the financial impact of both your organization and that of their customers. I find that this skill is tough to find in sales professionals today. There is a lot of pressure to generate revenue in order to make the top line of the business become a steep curve going north. The key, however, is to also understand profitability and investment made by the customer. Profitability is important because it gives you the necessary cash to sustain your business long term. Investments made by your customers in working with you should be looked at in the same way. That helps them solve their business problem in the most economical way for them, and is the most profitable for you in the long term.

135

> ### Epilogue
>
> *By understanding the common denominator of the sales transaction—exchange of dollars—your sales professionals will understand the impacts of that transaction for themselves, you, your organization, and their customers.*

111

Sales Performance and Productivity Must Equal Dollars Invested in New Business

I could reference hundreds of sales performance and productivity studies and include the Pareto principle to saythat 80 percent of your revenue comes from 20 percent of your top sales performers. I

> ### Assignment
>
> Make it a point to perform constant and continuous vigilance on your sales pipeline for new business. Also monitor the amount of time spent in trying to obtain new business.

could also reference the idea that it costs more to generate new business than it does to keep your current customers/clients and help them solve additional problems and generate additional business. This is all well documented. So now comes the time when you must help your sales professionals understand and make a decision on where they invest their time. It is very costly to invest in new business. Therefore, as you are making decisions on whether or not to invest in going after a new prospect, you must first have a detailed conversation with your sales professional about the amount of investment that needs to be made. This will ensure that the amount of time (assuming outstanding performance and productivity) equates to a large enough return on the investment made to secure the new business. There is a great allure to and motivational factor for acquiring more new business with new prospects. Sometimes it's worth the investment, and sometime you are spending too much time and money trying to obtain new business and a new customer.

Epilogue

Don't take your eye off the investment factor of trying to obtain new business.

112

Establish a Sales Process/ System and Stick to It

I've interviewed hundreds of sales professionals and managers, and most of them admit to not using a sales process and/ or system. I typically hear that "sales is an individual art and cannot be replicated," or "I have my own style and my sales techniques only work for me."

Assignment

Map your sales processes. Document all of the sales tasks, activities, decision points, and hand-offs that need to take place in order to close a deal and set up a customer to do business with your company.

Sometimes I hear, "I've tried a number of sales models I learned from my sales training through the years and nothing really sticks or is useful." My experience is that this is all hogwash!

I would argue that these are all excuses and "old school" reasons for not wanting to really understand and be held accountable to a sales process that can be measured for performance and improvement based on lessons learned and circumstances that need to change with the changing nature of your business and that of your customers. Establishing a sales process provides the structure and foundation for successful tasks, activities, and outcomes. This is not meant to limit a sales professional's ability to be successful or create more bureaucratic "red tape;" processes are meant to provide the guidance and direction necessary to successfully accomplish the task at hand. Processes also establish how the sales work is to be performed (meaning you can measure how successful you are).

Epilogue

Top-notch sales professionals want to know their lines of authority for making decisions and making things happen. Provide them the foundation and guidance by creating, documenting, and communicating your sales processes.

113

Use the 7 and Out Rule

So you are having a conversation about a prospect and the information included in your account management profile with one of your top sales professionals. You ask a lot of questions about the particular work and tasks that have been performed during the front end of your sales process (for example, prospecting). Your sales professional shares with you that he or she has met with the operations department person who seems to be the decision-maker, and also once with a subject matter expert in the procurement department. In addition to the face-to-face

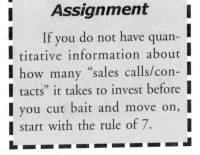

Assignment

If you do not have quantitative information about how many "sales calls/contacts" it takes to invest before you cut bait and move on, start with the rule of 7.

meetings, he or she has called several times for follow-up information and tried to schedule additional face-to-face meetings to review the committed next steps and action items. You then start to think of the amount of time invested, the number of meetings, the expense, and the worry about the lack of progress of getting to a close. In a qualitative way, I've uncovered from sales professionals that they use the "rule of 7." They will call on and work with a prospect an average of 7 times to determine whether there is a true buying signal and opportunity to move forward in the sales process. This is not an exact science. The number of client interactions will vary depending on what you are selling, the complexity of the sale, and the dollars involved in the sales transaction. You can at least judge where you are in the sales process, how much progress you've made, and the thoroughness of the information collected on the prospect, and then give counsel on the next steps to take.

Epilogue

Apply the rule of 7: Either move forward with the prospect or move on.

114

Hire Only Skilled and Competent Sales Managers/Leaders

So you are a sales manager and have managers and/or supervisors reporting to you. Assuming you have to add or replace a manager/supervisor, then your objective must be no different from hiring the best sales professional. I would add one critical recommendation, and that is to add the key skills and competencies

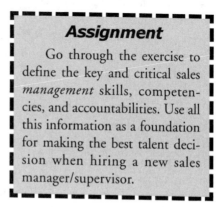

Assignment

Go through the exercise to define the key and critical sales *management* skills, competencies, and accountabilities. Use all this information as a foundation for making the best talent decision when hiring a new sales manager/supervisor.

necessary to be a top sales manager. There are different skills and competencies necessary to be successful in this role, so don't make the mistake of thinking and/or applying the sales skills and competencies and assume that translates into sales management.

Epilogue

Being a great sales professional doesn't always mean being a great sales manager.

115

Don't Promote Highly Competent Sales Professionals Into Management Unless They Are or Have the Potential to Be Good Leaders

We all hear the stories of a great sales performer who gets promoted in sales management and then fails miserably. It happens all the time. Why? For one, the succession process in most organizations is still based on a 1950s model of orga-

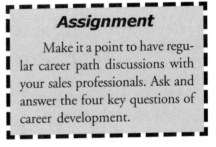

Assignment

Make it a point to have regular career path discussions with your sales professionals. Ask and answer the four key questions of career development.

nizational design and promotion. In other words, if you do a great job as a sales professional, then you will be considered for a managerial position and make more money. It boils down to title and more money rather than really leveraging a sales professional's strengths and career desires. When you are working with your sales professionals on career development, you must ask and have answered the following four questions:

1. Do you want to move up in the company?

2. Do you want to stay put?

3. Do you want to move laterally and take on responsibilities outside of sales?

4. Are your plans to move out of the organization?

Once you have asked and answered these questions, then you can determine the best direction for your sales professional based on his or her career aspirations and direction.

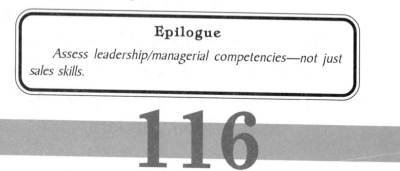

> **Epilogue**
>
> *Assess leadership/managerial competencies—not just sales skills.*

116

Have Your Top Executives Support Your Sales Efforts

I would never have dreamed that this topic needed to be included in this book. This should be a given, but, unfortunately, it isn't. The key word here is "support." And support begins with executives' understanding of the goals, objectives, and busi-

> **Assignment**
>
> After you've developed your sales plan, share this with your top executives for understanding and support for your plan of execution.

ness outcomes you expect to achieve. The reason I've included this here is because when there is "support," you have aligned your objectives, which enables you to cascade the sales goals and objectives to the rest of your sales team. When you are able to clearly document and articulate your sales objectives for your sales team, you provide a basis of understanding on where you are headed, what you need to accomplish, and how all performance will be measured. Once you achieve this alignment and are able to educate your sales team on the direction because you've obtained the top-down "support," this will provide the information needed to be highly motivated to accomplish the established goals and objectives. So share your plan, solicit feedback, and collaborate with your top executives. This will ensure that the direction in which you need to head in order to accomplish your objectives is aligned to the top executives expectations' and business strategy.

> **Epilogue**
>
> *Not getting executive "support" is like marching into war without a plan.*

117

Make Sales Recruiting a Priority for Executives and Top Sales Performers

This is a reflection of you as a top sales manager. In addition to being judged by your sales results and sales employee retention, you will also be judged by how and

> **Assignment**
>
> Obtain commitment on your selection process from your executives and top sales performers, and engage them in the process.

who you hire. Hiring is just as important as getting results and retention. You need to take this very seriously. The cost of hire is expensive, and the cost of a bad hire is even more expensive. The recruiting of top talent *must be a priority*. This needs to be a priority for you and it also needs to be a priority for your executives and top sales performers. In his book *Topgrading*, Bradford Smart quantifies the cost of mis-hires based on his research and case studies. This number can be staggering when you consider cost of hire, compensation, cost of maintaining the sales person in the job, severance, and cost of mistakes with customers. Because this is so important, I recommend that you include your executives and top sales performers in the sourcing, recruiting, interviewing, and decision-making process when you are trying to fill an open sales position.

So, if you want to hire top sales professionals, you must include your executives and top sales performers in the candidate evaluation and hiring processes. After you educate them on the use of competencies and a thorough screening process, their input will be invaluable to your decision to hire or not hire. Do this upfront.

Epilogue

Avoid the mistakes of losing a top talent and having to explain the cost of the hire and the cost of a mis-hire.

118

Take Field Trips to Noncompetitive Industries to Learn New Ways to Improve Sales

Highly competent and motivated sales professionals love to learn new ideas and new ways to improve their performance. They innately have the desire to learn and comprehend how to improve. Leverage this by including in your team's

Assignment

Schedule a noncompetitive field trip outside your industry. Make this a shared learning experience for your sales professionals.

development the opportunity to meet and talk with well-recognized "noncompetitive" companies and peers to share information about what makes them unique and successful in their sales process. Sometimes getting a different point of view triggers an idea and/or thought that can greatly enhance sales performance. This is not to say that this exercise is about adopting new sales processes, but it is about learning and being able to adapt new ideas and ways in which to improve sales performance.

Epilogue

Great sales ideas don't have to be organic. Sometimes great ideas for sales process and individual improvement come from getting out of your silo and expanding your learning in noncompetitive ways.

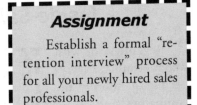

119

Conduct Retention Interviews With Newly Hired Sales Professionals

Most organizations conduct "exit interviews." Although some of the information is useful after a sales professional leaves your organization, most of the information is either not candid or poisoned with ill will

> **Assignment**
>
> Establish a formal "retention interview" process for all your newly hired sales professionals.

and bad feelings. I recommend an alternative—"retention interviews" with your sales professionals. What is a retention interview? A retention interview is a formal discussion with your newly hired sales professionals that is conducted 30 days, 90 days, and one

145

year from his or her date of hire. You would be amazed at the information you can collect and use to improve your sales area—everything from supervisor communications, relationships with peers and coworkers, and developmental needs. Here's a unique idea: How about you focus your energy on why your hired sales professionals are staying with you? Build on the information and all the good things that are going on in your organization.

> ### Epilogue
>
> *Why wait until a sales professional leaves the company in order to learn what went wrong?*

120

Set the Organizational Expectation That Everyone in the Company Has Responsibility for Sales, Not Just Outside- and Inside-Sales Teams

Regardless of with whom I consult, I always ask the question of the company's leadership, "Who is responsible for sales?" The answer is, of course, "Our sales team!" Think about this for a minute. Is this really true? Companies have to sell their products

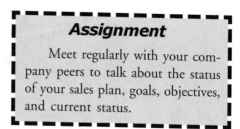

Assignment

Meet regularly with your company peers to talk about the status of your sales plan, goals, objectives, and current status.

and services in order to make money and a profit, right? Then if we follow that logic, everyone in the organization plays some part in making that happen, right? So if we need to sell in order to make money, and we need people to make this happen, wouldn't it be logical that everyone has a contribution in the company to make a sale? I think so. So, as the sales manager, you need to ensure that organizational expectations are communicated and that everyone understands roles, responsibilities, and accountabilities in order to grow your business. While your sales team is on the front end of the sales transaction until you close a deal, the rest of the organization has to support what is sold, including great customer service.

Not everyone has a sales title, and the intent of this Quick Idea is not to say that everyone is in the sales function. What this is intended to do is for you to ensure, through your proactive sales communications, that you are all playing the same game of business.

> ### Epilogue
> *The ultimate goal is to increase your sales on a regular and sustainable basis.*

121

Know All Your Sales Professionals By Name

Many organizations today are large and maybe even dispersed geographically. It's a tough job when you are a sales manager with a large sales staff. And it's especially difficult to say you know everyone by name. Even if you have just a handful of direct reports, you should ensure that you know all your team members' names by heart. People like to be recognized by their names—not by whom they report to, in what division they work, or where in the world they work. At the end of the

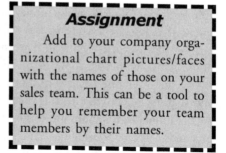

Assignment

Add to your company organizational chart pictures/faces with the names of those on your sales team. This can be a tool to help you remember your team members by their names.

day, this is a respectful way and a motivational way to let your team know that you care enough about them to know who they are. Your name has an emotional attachment to it. If your boss knows who you are, then you feel good about your relationship and connection to the company. If your boss does not know your name, you may wonder if you are relevant.

Epilogue

Make everyone relevant on your team by knowing who they are.

122

Get to Know the Sales Professional's Husband/Wife/ Significant Other

Typically, I find that high-achieving sales professionals do not become successful by themselves. The professional who is working for you is also influenced in his or her thought process and behavior by a spouse or significant other. These are the people who, when there is an outstanding relationship, become the "sounding boards and creative talent" behind the curtain of everyday professional lives. They hear the good, the bad, and the ugly. My wife is not

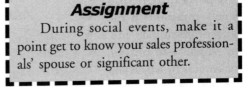

Assignment

During social events, make it a point get to know your sales professionals' spouse or significant other.

only my best friend, but she is also my best advisor on business situations. She doesn't know all the ins and outs of what I do for a living, but she listens to my problems and provides an objective view that gives me perspective on how to solve my business problems. This is highly productive and motivating. I hope you're as fortunate as I am.

Epilogue

Your sales professionals are human beings, and they are influenced by many people in order for them to be successful.

Get to Know the Sales Professional's Family

There are several organizations I know of that make a point to not only make hiring decisions but also promotional decisions based on understanding family dynamics. I am not suggesting either of these two methods, but what I am suggesting is that your sales professionals are human beings with family dynamics. In addition to their personal behaviors and attributes, they also come to work for you with family dynamics that make them who they are on any given day. Similar to reinforcing the motivational factor of understanding their clients and their business, so should you take the time to understand their family and friends. This will not only give you great insight into what's going on in the sales professional's life, but it will also provide the context by which you can address situations that may arise that may impact an individual's overall performance (for example, having to care for elderly parents, dealing with teenagers, or arranging child care).

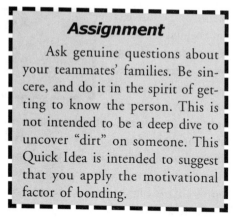

Assignment

Ask genuine questions about your teammates' families. Be sincere, and do it in the spirit of getting to know the person. This is not intended to be a deep dive to uncover "dirt" on someone. This Quick Idea is intended to suggest that you apply the motivational factor of bonding.

Epilogue

It can be helpful to get to know your sales team members on a deeper level.

124

Send the Spouse or Significant Other a Thank-You Note for His/ Her Contributions

In additional to individual sales performance while working for you, there is another ingredient to that success that I bet you didn't think about—the contributions and sacrifices made by your sales professional's spouse or significant other. Sales is a tough career. Some people don't realize the challenges that come with a sales career—travel and all its hassles today, being away from the family and missing family events, assisting when there is a home-front situation that needs to be addressed, child care, school—the list goes on and on. Recognizing these important people in your sales professionals' lives can go a long way in bridging the long hours, long days,

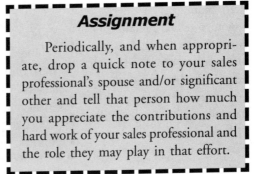

Assignment

Periodically, and when appropriate, drop a quick note to your sales professional's spouse and/or significant other and tell that person how much you appreciate the contributions and hard work of your sales professional and the role they may play in that effort.

and grueling schedules. Recognize the contributions that are made by the spouse or significant other to the success of your sale professionals.

Epilogue
Understand how hard the work/life balance is for everyone, not just your sales professional.

125

Show Your Emotion and Passion About Sales

As a sales manager and leader, you must positively demonstrate your emotions and passions about your industry, your company, your plan, and your people. A study conducted by Nohria, Groysberg, and Lee and reported in Harvard Business Review revealed that organizations don't have an absolute monopoly on employee motivation or on fulfilling employees' emotional drives. As the sales professional manager, you matter too. Employees expect their managers to do their best to provide direction, be enthusiastic about the sales plan and the people who will execute the plan, the culture, opportunities, and overall financial performance of the organization.

> **Assignment**
>
> Demonstrate through your communications and behaviors, whether on a call, by e-mail, and/or in a meeting, that you have passion about your business, plan, and people.

> **Epilogue**
>
> *You must show your passion about what you and your team are accountable to deliver. If you don't have passion or can't demonstrate that passion, you need to find another career.*

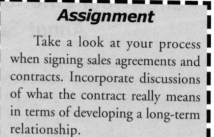

126

Build Customer Relationships With Mutual Trust, Not Just a Contract

The point of this Quick Idea is to not forget the fact that, although it's your sales professional's job to secure an agreement to "close the deal," it does not have to be a win/lose situation. In my interviews with customers in evaluating customer experiences, there is this sense in some sales transactions that they need

> **Assignment**
>
> Take a look at your process when signing sales agreements and contracts. Incorporate discussions of what the contract really means in terms of developing a long-term relationship.

the product and/or service, and that's what it's *all* about—just the signing of the contract. I would recommend that the contract really should be represented as a summation of your understanding of their business problems and how you are going to provide products and/or services to resolve them. This will also include pricing and boilerplate legal information. Approaching sales contracts and agreements in this manner gives your sales professionals an opportunity to foster a key driver of developing that deep customer relationship that accounts for the enormous boost of motivation. Use this as a means to coach and guide your sales professionals to work with their customers to understand your best intentions and service. This will have a dramatic impact on your sales professionals to build a relationship even when they are closing the deal and having to obtain signatures for formal contracts and agreements.

Epilogue

Contracts and agreements should be used for building bonds and long-term relationships with your customers and clients.

127

Listen to Your Team

As a sales manager, while you are in the position to make critical business decisions, don't overlook the accountability to really listen to your sales team. Treat your team members just as you would if they were your customers. Not only is this a critical skill, but it is also tied to your

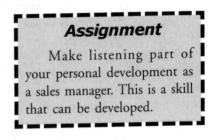

Assignment

Make listening part of your personal development as a sales manager. This is a skill that can be developed.

sales team motivation in wanting to culturally fit and connect to their boss. When you effectively listen to your team, you accomplish several key motivating factors. This fosters mutual friendship among your team members, creates a working atmosphere of collaboration and teamwork, and encourages the sharing of great ideas and creative resolutions to solving business problems. Listening to your team begins with your undivided attention during conversations. There is a strong tie between your ability to really listen to your sales professionals and their motivation to align to your expectations and organizational culture.

> **Epilogue**
> *You have two ears but just one mouth...for a reason.*

128

Listen to Your Customer

What did you say? All humor aside, listening is a critical sales skill. My experience is that we think we do a good job of really listening to our custom-

Assignment

Teach and reinforce the importance of great listening skills with your sales professionals.

ers, but we don't. On a personal and professional level, we are so busy with what we want to say that we really fail to listen. I've reviewed hundreds of formal customer feedback surveys, and the number-one item that stands out either in a great way or a horrible way is the experience of listening between the sales professional and his or her customer. Whether the customer is happy or unhappy, he or she wants to be heard, and this person determines whether he or she will conduct business with you based on your sales professional's ability to listen, learn, and understand the customer's business problems.

Every sales training session you have attended and book you've read identifies and reinforces the fact that great listening skills are important. The key is not only to have these skills, but when you really apply them it gives the sales professional greater opportunity to bond with a customer and comprehend his or her business problems. This is highly motivating for a top sales performer.

Epilogue

Everyone wants to be listened to.

129

Move the Cheese

Have you ever read the book *Who Moved My Cheese?* by Spencer Johnson (G.P. Putnam's Sons, 1998)? What an easy read about an amazing way to deal with

Assignment

Make it a practice to move the cheese. Read the book *Who Moved My Cheese?* and apply the underlying principles to your sales professionals.

change in your work and in your life. As the sales manager, you know that changes occur annually, monthly, weekly, daily, and hourly. So why not tap into the energy that change creates and use it as a tool to help motivate your sales professionals? Why would I want to create more change knowing that the sales team deals with change every day? The answer is you are not going to create change for change's sake. What you need to do is, when things are not aligning to meet your overall sales goals and objectives, think about making a few changes (for example, obtaining feedback on a stalled deal from a team member who is not close to the deal, assigning a tough client to a high-potential sales professional, or insert a subject matter expert into a sales transaction in order to close the deal). Sales professionals deal with change on a regular and consistent basis. When you do move the cheese you will be tapping into a great motivational factor: You will be increasing the ability to accept change in an easier way and build trust by coaching your sales professionals through the change.

Epilogue

Sometimes you need to change your technique, learn a new way, and apply it to get a different result.

130

Exercise, and Set Expectations for Your Team to Keep Physically Fit

One sales manager told me in a coaching session that the day-to-day tasks and activities just wear her down. We had a conversation not only about the tasks to be tackled and completed but about her routine that prepares her for the tough tasks. I asked her about the amount of time necessary to accomplish her daily routines, and came to find out that, in addition to all the work, travel, and keeping

---

Assignment

Make it a routine to work out and keep physically fit. Also, be sure you emphasize the importance of this to your sales professionals.

---

the team focused, she did not carve out time for herself to exercise. She was a former athlete and competitor, and you could tell this by her motivation and performance. The challenge was for her to get more energy and be sharp during the day. So I suggested that, just like scheduling time for client meetings, she should carve out time for herself to get back into the routine to exercise every morning and begin the process to keep physically fit.

Epilogue

When you keep yourself physically fit you have more energy to be a top performer.

131

Establish the "No Asshole" Rule

What is the "No Asshole" rule? First, the name is a book written by Robert Sutton, PhD, *The No Asshole Rule* (Business Plus, 2007). Second, it's a cultural guide to ensure you have clear expectations of acceptable behavior. As the sales manager, it is your job to provide the

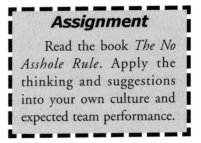

Assignment

Read the book *The No Asshole Rule*. Apply the thinking and suggestions into your own culture and expected team performance.

"rules of the game" for teamwork, collaboration, and interaction (internally and externally) with your customers. Admittedly, sales professionals have to have a sense of ego. This ego, however, doesn't have to be one that demonstrates personal insults, threats and intimidation, flaming e-mails, status slaps in public, rude interruptions, and treating people like they are invisible. As the sales manager, it is your job to set the behavioral expectations of your team, and the "no asshole" rules that are non-negotiable and unacceptable.

> ### Epilogue
> *It's your job as the sales manager to set the tone and culture of what is acceptable behavior.*

132

Solicit Sales Help From Key Internal Sponsors

Did you know your sales professionals are already soliciting help from key people within your organization during the sales process? Top-notch sales professionals don't hesitate to reach out to key contributors and people

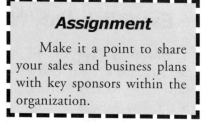

Assignment

Make it a point to share your sales and business plans with key sponsors within the organization.

they trust who can help them collaborate and close a deal. It's a great opportunity to take the lead and proactively provide direction to your sales team about how to engage your internal key sponsors in order to facilitate and support the closing of any deal. This typically includes providing key information and also insights into competitive information that might be helpful for the sales professional during the sales cycle. This will help a sales professional calibrate how he or she can go about aligning customer requests for information and internal subject matter expertise, which includes internal people who have a skill and passion for helping the business continue to grow and generate revenue.

You never know what a prospect or customer might want in terms of getting comfortable with your organization in order to do business with you. It might take a subject matter expert outside your sales organization to close a deal. Ensure that it's okay to do this with your sales team. They will be glad you set the expectations upfront and understand the approach on how to leverage your internal resources to help close deals.

> **Epilogue**
> *Leverage internal resources to help close deals.*

133

Create an Atmosphere in Which It's Okay to Fail and Learn

Here's a little secret that you will not find in other sales and business development books: The secret of continuous sales success as a sales manager is to create an environment of continuous learning so that your sales professionals learn how to do what they don't

Assignment

Make it clear that no one is perfect, and that what you care about is the effort it takes to learn, and apply that learning to improve individual and team performance.

know how to do. Every sales manager with whom I've worked says one of the key management and leadership challenges is to create an atmosphere in which it's okay to fail and take the lessons learned when things do not work out in a sales transaction. Sales professionals have a strong desire to succeed, but they also have a balanced approach to making changes in their skills from their learning.

159

> **Epilogue**
> *Bet on learners on your sales team. They will drive for results based on a strong desire to improve their performance.*

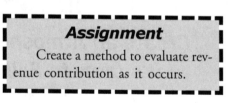

Don't Expecting a Normal Distribution of Revenue From Your Sales Team

Let's face the facts. There are those who want to do well and sometimes outperform others on the sales team. You count on your "A"

> **Assignment**
> Create a method to evaluate revenue contribution as it occurs.

players to deliver sustainable and consistent sales results. Your "B" players will fluctuate in regard to their performance and contributions to sales revenue. And your "C" players will be all over the board when you measure their performance and contributions to all of your sales goals and objectives. Although you might expect a normal distribution of sales performance as it relates to revenue generation by your sales team, don't be surprised that you might have a wide distribution that is weighted toward your "A" players and varies depending on the performance of your "B" and "C" players. Fluctuations in sales and business cycles will need to be measured throughout multiple periods of time. If you hire and retain top-notch sales professionals, your normal distribution will be skewed toward the left of the typical distribution curve. This is exactly want you want to work toward as a sales manager.

Epilogue

Expecting that you will find a normal distribution of revenue contribution may lead to suprises.

Do Everything You Can to Keep Your "A" Sales Contributors

This is completely obvious to any sales manager: Keep your "A" contributors. They produce the majority of your revenue. There is an exception, and I bet you didn't think I was going to go

> **Assignment**
>
> Always monitor sales performance and tie the sales performance to great sales teamwork behaviors.

here, but if an "A" sales contributor defies your authority, breaks company policies, and/or disrupts your team mission or direction, then that person must go—regardless of his or her contribution. Such behavior is not only disruptive to your goals and objectives, but your other sales team members also are watching it. If you allow this behavior into your team for the sake of meeting your sales targets, I guarantee your success will be short-lived. You will also lose your other "A" contributors because they will see you don't have the backbone to deal with a disruptive "A" contributor.

Remember, there can be two kinds of "A" sales contributors: one who exceeds his/her sales goals and objectives and has a great teamwork and a collaborative spirit, and one who exceeds his/her sales goals but disrupts the overall team effort. You must address the latter or your credibility as a sales manager will be questioned.

Epilogue

Money isn't everything—behavior is.

Check Your Ego At the Door

The traditional approach to sales professional math on closing the deal (big ego + smooth talker + nice suit = Big Sale) just doesn't cut it anymore. Why? Times have changed. Let's not discount that

Assignment

Change your attitude about your role as a sale manager. It's now your time to make sure your ego does not get into the way of great coaching and mentoring.

fact that sales professionals are told "no" millions of times a day. They need the reassurance that you, as their sales manager, understand that they get rejected on a recurring basis. Because you understand what it's like to be in that position, you will need to look at your own ego and make sure that your focus is on assisting them while they are being rejected. Although it is a sales professional's motivation to bond with customers and clients to feel as though he or she is driving toward sales contribution, you must not let your ego get in the way of rescuing your sales professional when he or she is going through the everyday rejection process.

Epilogue

If you are arrogant and distant, then expect the same from your sales professionals. If you are motivational, your team will respond in kind.

137

It's Okay to Sweat, but Maintain Your Composure

I've found that, outside of the sales profession, people really don't understand that, if sales professionals don't do a great job, they might not be able to feed themselves or their families. I've also uncovered that operational, administrative, and other roles

> ### Assignment
>
> When you feel the need to take a break because the pressure is mounting, listen to your gut and take that break. Don't bust someone's chops just because you are frustrated.

within the organization have the perception that sales is about partying and playing golf. Based on my work assessing hundreds of development competencies, the top players work hard, don't party too much, and most of the time don't have time to play golf. So when the going gets tough and you've done an outstanding job in hiring "A" players, know that they are working hard to reach your goals and objectives. They will be motivated by the fact that they have something to defend: your loyalty, their jobs, and the continued success of the organization. Your sales professionals decided to work for you when you hired them, and they keep working hard for you because you care about them. Even when the heat gets turned up from your boss, a customer, or an internal political situation, always remember to try not to let your team see you sweat, and always maintain your composure as a leader.

> ### Epilogue
> *It is okay to let them see you sweat—just be cool about it!*

138

Hope Does Not Close Deals

In the book *Hope Is Not a Strategy*, by Rick Page, he talks about the complexity of today's sales process. Specifically he talks about why it's

> ### Assignment
> Read the book *Hope Is Not a Strategy*, by Rick Page.

so difficult for sales professionals to get an accurate understanding of where they are in a complex sale, including not hoping that a buyer is going to buy from you. The bottom line is that it's to the customer's advantage to keep the sales professional in the dark about key and critical information in order to save the information while trying to negotiate a deal. The point is that, as a sales manager, you need to coach your sales professionals so that they have the courage to uncover the necessary information in order for you and your potential business partner to make the best decision on the sales transaction. This includes taking the time and effort to work through a thorough due-diligence process, finding the decision-maker(s), determining budget to fix the business problem or purchase a product, and uncovering their buying patterns. Are they low-price buyers or are they more savvy in their procurement and understand the total cost of sale? Effective sales professionals drive to uncover, gather, and comprehend all the relevant customer information necessary to fix a business problem for a customer. Don't let "hope" creep into your sales process.

> ### Epilogue
> *Top-notch sales professionals do their homework.*

139

Maintain Your Sense of Humor

Times are tough. It's more competitive in your market than ever before. You have pressure from your boss to meet and exceed your sales num-

> ### *Assignment*
>
> Try to find the humor in everything—sometimes it's hidden, but it's there.

bers. Your customers are complaining that you've had to raise your prices due the huge increase in fuel costs. You have pressure to maintain a work/life balance and you are sandwiched between having kids who need your attention and elderly parents who have health problems. What is a sales leader supposed to do and how does this relate to maintaining a highly motivated sales team? This reminds me of the movie *Saving Private Ryan* starring Tom Hanks. I'll never forget the scene when Tom was sitting in the half-demolished chapel sharing his concerns and thoughts about their situation with his sergeant named Frank. While he was sharing his thoughts about their situation and plans for the next day, his hand was shaking when he grabbed a cup of water. He was under so much pressure and he was unsure about the events of the upcoming day's mission. He then cracked a joke, seemed too ease, for the moment, Sergeant Frank's uneasiness. That moment had an effect on Sergeant Frank in a positive way. He understood his boss was human and that they had a hard mission ahead of them the next day. All that seriousness was peppered with a little sense of humor.

165

> **Epilogue**
> *Humor has a way of diffusing stressful situations during tough times.*

140

Clear the Way for Streamlined Internal Decision-Making

Nothing is worse to a highly motivated sales professional than going through internal "red tape" to get a decision made during a sales transaction. The best process that I can recommend is to have expectations about the types of

> **Assignment**
>
> Establish, explain, and set expectations with your sales team that internal decision-making about sales transactions follows an internal process and efficient decision-making flow.

decisions that need to be decided during any sales transaction based on your business, whether you are selling products or services. When you say, "my business is unique, the sales process is fluid, and, based on how we close deals, I can't come up with every scenario or possible decision that might be made during a sales transaction," I disagree. If you know your business, then the type of sales transactions you encounter, you know the type of objections you get from your customers, and the challenges you have on pricing and approvals during the transaction. Once you have established the internal decision-making protocol for a sales transaction within your organization, get out of the way and let your sales professionals handle the internal discussions in order to close deals.

166

> ### Epilogue
> *Be the coach and not the bottleneck.*

141

Be a Visible and Accessible Sales Leader

Your sales team wants to experience that their leader is engaged and genuinely interested in their successes. What does this mean? It means more than an open-door policy. It also means more than just showing up to con-

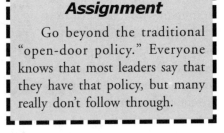

Assignment

Go beyond the traditional "open-door policy." Everyone knows that most leaders say that they have that policy, but many really don't follow through.

duct performance evaluations on an annual basis or only attending the annual sales event. As a leader, you need to be available physically or by phone and/or e-mail when your sales professionals are in a jam and need to problem-solve. This means that when a sales professional has a conflict with a customer concerning a purchase order or payment, he or she should know he or she can pick up the phone and get advice on how to handle the situation.

> ### Epilogue
> *If you really want highly motivated sales professionals and followers that bust their butts to accomplish their objectives and grow your business, become a highly visible and accessible sales leader.*

142

Manage Natural Internal Conflicts Between Sales and Operations

Whether you believe this or not, natural internal conflicts exist between sales and operations. Differing perceptions exist from the two functional areas of any business, large or small. Sales professionals are given expectations, goals, and objectives to acquire more clients, generate more revenue, and sustain

> ### Assignment
>
> Practice the art of coaching your sales team to understand that collaboration with your operations professionals is in the best interests of meeting your commitments.

customer relationships. Operations professionals, however, are expected to produce the products and/or services and provide the structure that the business needs to operate in an effective manner. Sometimes those objectives conflict. For example, a sales professional makes a commitment to a customer to provide a product and/or solution on a particular date without checking with operations to determine if they can meet that commitment. Maybe operations doesn't have the capacity or resources, and are in the middle of an audit from an outside regulatory agency. You are in a pickle, my friend. You now have a huge conflict. Your sales professional made a commitment that you now cannot deliver, the operations team is mad because they would like to plan and be able deliver.

When you have multiple people and departments involved in sales transactions, ensure you are managing the natural internal conflicts that exist because of competing priorities. Be a good sales leader and take this in the course of outstanding service and meeting your commitments.

> **Epilogue**
> *Keep in mind that your actions can affect others.*
> *Collaborate!*

143

Don't Take Over a Sales Call

Let's make the assumption that you've trained and educated your sales team to perform at a high level on a sales call. Let's also make the assumption that you are participating in a sales call for the purposes of engaging your customer/client and obtaining information to coach and further develop a sales professional. Let's also assume that during the call, the meeting starts to take a direction that you didn't anticipate and you need to make adjustments on the fly. *Fight the urge* to jump in and rescue your sales professional. There is nothing more demotivating than having your boss jump in and be the hero in order to save the day and fix the situation. This not only creates a dynamic with your sales professionals that makes them feel inadequate, but it also gives your customers and/or clients the perception that the sales professionals with whom they are dealing cannot fend for themselves or make decisions

> **Assignment**
> While you conduct joint sales calls with your sales professionals, set up the expectation as part of your preparation for the meeting that you are there to add value to the meeting and that the leadership and decision-making for the meeting rests with the sales professional.

169

in order to solve a situation or business problem that is being addressed.

> ## Epilogue
> *Fight the urge to insert yourself.*

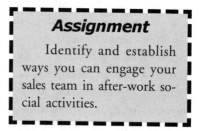

Provide After-Work Activities With Coworkers

This is not intended to be the "happy hour club" at the local pub. In today's world of risks and liability, when the company and/or the company representative supports and/or pays for an evening of adult beverages, be prepared to have

> **Assignment**
>
> Identify and establish ways you can engage your sales team in after-work social activities.

your human resources and legal beagles schedule a talk with you. Another risk you have as the sales manager is the alienation of team members that do not imbibe alcoholic beverages. There are creative ways to engage the social bonding that is required in order to keep your sales team engaged with your organization and your sales team.

So find these creative ways to engage your sales team in after-work activities. Although it's great when everyone participates, don't make it mandatory or even give the impression that "you must participate." Otherwise, you will not be part of the team. Work/life balance is important, and some of your sales professionals have family obligations after work. Do this in the spirit of bringing your team together so they get to know their teammates better.

Epilogue

Social bonding is important. Just be smart about how you get there.

145

Celebrate Wins

What's the use of putting in all the hard work to close deals and grow the business unless you can celebrate your wins? Celebrating wins can be as simple as a phone call from the sales manager to the sales professional who just closed the deal to say great job, or it can more elaborate by bringing together your sales team and reviewing the wins you've had during a period of time. The DNA of top-notch sales professionals hardwires them to work hard to solve their customers' business problems, add value, make a difference, be recognized for a job well done, and be well compensated...in that order.

Assignment

Begin the managerial practice of day-to-day feedback on great sales performance. Pick up the phone and call and congratulate your top performers with their wins on a daily basis.

I knew a sales pro who kept a cooler in his truck when he met with the prospect and they were near a deal. Once the deal closes, he opened the truck and opened a bottle of his favorite sparkling wine to toast his win that day (non-alcoholic may be your preference). Keep in mind that even the top performers need a pat on the back and recognition to celebrate their wins. This needs to occur on a regular basis, with sincerity.

Epilogue

Motivation and continuous improvement in the sales process can't wait until annual review time and/or sales meetings.

146

Include Customer Feedback in Product/Service Development and Give Credit to Sales Professionals Who Bring Back This Information

It only makes good business sense to collect, evaluate, and put into your product/service development the feedback from your customers. An engaged sales team will be motivated to collect such valuable information because they see the benefits of improvement. This gives them continued competitive advantage when it comes to improving their current customers' situations, and allows them more opportunities to solve new prospects' business problems. By involving your sales team in continuous improvement, they will take ownership of the improvements made to products and services and will be passionate about delivering the value to new prospects. This also gives the sales professional the opportunity to use additional customer experiences as evidence that your organization really cares about helping solve customer problems. It also hits home the notion that the relationship is not just a sales transaction but also a business partnership. This adds great sales leverage and value, for the sales professional, the organization, and the customer.

> **Assignment**
>
> Develop a formal method to collect and evaluate customer feedback for product/service improvement. Instruct your sales team to use this method to obtain a better understanding of the changing dynamics of your customers' business.

When you put into play a method to allow your sales professional to collect, analyze, and provide customer feedback, this will not only improve the connection that you have with your sales team, but will also provide added benefit ofproviding your sales professionals with a valuable tool in customer references.

> **Epilogue**
> *Motivation for improvement comes from business partnerships and the constructive feedback to improve.*

147

Provide Company Logo Apparel to Wear When Meeting With Customers/Clients/Community

This goes beyond just a company logo. It's your brand. Top-notch sales professionals are proud people. When they really believe in the products and services they represent, they like to show it off. Company logoed apparel is noticeable in today's work environment. When your brand is recognizable, your customers and prospects will associate the sales professional with his

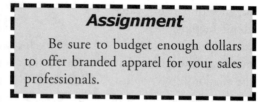

Assignment

Be sure to budget enough dollars to offer branded apparel for your sales professionals.

or her organization. When you have a strong brand, this will be reflected in the sales professionals that represent it, and your customers/prospects will recognize and connect your brand to your sales professionals who wear your logo. Think about giving your customers your branded apparel too. Many of them will wear the clothing, making them walking billboards on your behalf! In today's business environment, the dress policies are business usually casual, but some organizations still have the expectation at the C-suite level that a suit and tie is appropriate work attire. In the business-casual situation, provide oxford shirts with your logo. Also consider professional golf shirts and light outdoor jackets. If the work environment is formal, consider suit-jacket lapel pins. Your sales professionals will wear this with great pride, and your customers will connect your brand and logo with the outstanding service your sales professionals provide.

Epilogue

Provide ways for your sales professionals to show their pride in their organization.

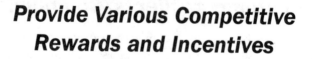

148

Provide Various Competitive Rewards and Incentives

Remember that base salary is entry into the game when you are hiring and retaining top sales talent. After satisfying the need for a competitive base salary, sales professionals want to be rewarded for extraordinary performance. In other words,

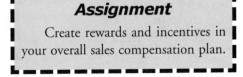

Assignment

Create rewards and incentives in your overall sales compensation plan.

when you go above and beyond and contribute to the overall success of the sales objectives, sales professionals want to see the fruits of their labor. This also enables you as the sales manager to really reward top performance. Compensation never should be delivered in a "socialistic" manner such that everyone gets the same base pay and incentive rewards. You need to figure out how to incentivize and reward top performance.

Epilogue

Incentives work.

149

Share a Salesperson's Accomplishments With His/Her Peers

Recognition is a huge motivator. In the course of your business, keep abreast of the day-to-day and specific above-and-beyond accomplishments of your sales professionals. Accomplishments can be as simple as handling a customer compliant and as significant as closing a "mega deal." When a sales manager makes the effort to share accomplishments with his/her peers, two things happen with regard to motivation:

1. The individual being recognized for the accomplishment has the feeling that he or she is making a contribution to the organization and team.

2. Peers take in the situation with a little bit of jealousy, which, for mature sales professionals, gives them a positive motivation to be recognized by their boss for a job well done.

> **Assignment**
>
> Practice the art of providing regular recognition when you gather your team for informal and formal sales meetings.

> **Epilogue**
> *When you provide recognition for a job well done, you are hitting on two very important human drivers of performance and motivation: the desire do a good job and the feeling of accomplishment.*

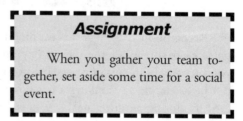

150

Throw a Party

Most sales professionals are social creatures. Parties, big and small, allow for social interaction and the chance for the sales professional to learn more about the people with whom they work.

> **Assignment**
>
> When you gather your team together, set aside some time for a social event.

The information gathered by sales professionals about the other people with whom they work is a valuable resource that top-notch sales professionals use to size up people. The information gathered is not negative. Salespeople believe they have a knack for sizing up people, and use this information to develop deeper relationships with those with whom they are working and networking.

Don't underestimate the value of social events such as throwing a party. In today's business environment, some organizations have policies in place about serving alcohol; alcohol doesn't have to be included as part of the party—certainly you can be creative and plan a little fun and socialization without it.

Epilogue

Sales professionals work hard and play hard. That's how they are wired.

151

Provide Competitive Compensation

This is entry into the game. Remember that sales professionals are motivated by the behaviors to acquire, close deals, and help you grow your business. It's imperative in today's competitive environment, for top-notch talent, that you continually monitor the labor market regarding compensation. Understand

Assignment

Do your own research. Check out Internet-based compensation sources. Also, make it a point to regularly meet with your human resources and/or compensation department to ensure that your sales compensation plan is competitive.

that your sales professionals have as much information about what competitive pay is as does your compensation department. If you want to hire and keep top-notch sales talent you will have to put your money where your mouth is.

Epilogue
Don't be cheap. You get what you pay for.

Index

About the Authors

Frank R. Horvath is a solutions architect and principal consultant for The Newman Group, a Futurestep and Korn Ferry Company. He has served a wide range of industries and clients in the areas of strategic talent management, including expertise in: performance management, recruiting, competency assessment, development, and retention. Mr. Horvath also has experience in sale force assessment, deployment and technology implementation, organizational effectiveness, business process improvement, workforce planning, project management, change management, operations management, and strategic financial planning. He has helped his clients effectively develop and execute sales strategies and business strategies, and improve sales performance.

Prior to The Newman Group, Mr. Horvath was president of Integrated Group Synergy, LLC. IGS, LLC provided talent management consulting services to a variety of business and industries. Additional executive leadership experience includs ADESA, Inc., where he was the director of HR talent and systems management, and Black & Veatch for which he was the managing director of the supply chain and management consulting practices.

151 Quick Ideas to Motivate Your Sales Force

Julie Vincent, APR, has more than 25 years of experience in corporate communications, media relations, crisis management, marketing, and writing services. She is president and owner of Wordsmith Communications Group, Inc., a full-service marketing communications consulting firm, and a public relations consultant on Diabetes Care for Roche Diagnostics.

Right out of college, Julie taught journalism, English, speech, and creative writing on the secondary level, and still holds a lifetime teaching license in the state of Indiana. She is currently an adjunct professor at IUPUI in the Journalism department.

A published author and a national award-winning corporate communicator, Julie has a B.S. in journalism, English, and radio/television/film from Ball State University and a M.S. in Journalism and secondary education from Butler University. She also has her APR designation from the Public Relations Society of America and is a past president of both the Hoosier Chapter of PRSA and the Indianapolis Public Relations Society.

Julie, her husband Dave, and their son Gavin live in Indianapolis.